Making Surveys Work
for Your Library

MAKING SURVEYS WORK FOR YOUR LIBRARY

Guidance, Instructions, and Examples

Robin Miller and Kate Hinnant

LIBRARIES UNLIMITED™

An Imprint of ABC-CLIO, LLC

Santa Barbara, California • Denver, Colorado

Library of Congress Cataloging-in-Publication Data

Names: Miller, Robin, 1980– author. | Hinnant, Kate, 1970– author.
Title: Making surveys work for your library : guidance, instructions, and examples / Robin Miller and Kate Hinnant.
Description: Santa Barbara, California : Libraries Unlimited, [2019] | Includes bibliographical references and index.
Identifiers: LCCN 2018033823 (print) | LCCN 2018042586 (ebook) | ISBN 9781440861086 (ebook) | ISBN 9781440861079 (pbk. : acid-free paper)
Subjects: LCSH: Library surveys. | Library administration—Decision making.
Classification: LCC Z678 (ebook) | LCC Z678 .M49 2019 (print) | DDC 025.5/8—dc23
LC record available at https://lccn.loc.gov/2018033823

ISBN: 978-1-4408-6107-9 (paperback)
      978-1-4408-6108-6 (ebook)

23 22 21 20 19   1 2 3 4 5

This book is also available as an e-book.

Libraries Unlimited
An Imprint of ABC-CLIO, LLC

ABC-CLIO, LLC
130 Cremona Drive, P.O. Box 1911
Santa Barbara, CA 93116-1911
www.abc-clio.com

This book is printed on acid-free paper ∞

Manufactured in the United States of America

For John Pollitz:
"What do they mean? It's not that cold in here."

Contents

Acknowledgments

Thank you to our colleagues and friends at McIntyre Library and the University of Wisconsin–Eau Claire. If you are bemused by our enthusiasm for surveys, you are gracious editors, testers, and analysts. Thank you, also, to our survey respondents—you have taught us more than you know.

A special thanks to our director, Jill Markgraf, for supporting us in this project. And to our colleagues Hans Kishel, Eric Jennings, and Jenna Vande Zande, for stepping in for us when we needed to work on this book.

The Value of Surveys, and Why They're Hard to Get Right

The 21st-century culture of librarianship is responsive and innovative; we strive to be indispensable. Librarian of Congress Dr. Carla D. Hayden, responding to a question about all the things that libraries do to serve their users, noted that "the most crucial skill" of a librarian is "the ability to be open, to learn new things." In the broader context of technological, demographic, and budgetary changes, we gain insights into the populations we serve by asking questions that measure the present and anticipate the future. To create the libraries our patrons need, librarians are continuously learning about our users.

And we have a large constellation of library-user information, ranging from conversations with individuals, to analysis of collection usage data, to reports published by professional associations and government agencies. Surveys fit into this undertaking as one of the most efficient means of gathering information directly from library users. The best surveys offer insights that we can gain only by asking our users questions that they alone can answer. The following questions illuminate what library users do, think, want, and feel:

When deciding to attend a program, please rank the importance of the following:

Day of the week
Time of the program

Transportation available

Program topic

Please rate your satisfaction with our chat service.

What other public spaces should be added to our library?

How long are you willing to wait for a book to become available on Overdrive?

As a large-scale research method, surveys allow us to look at a question through a wide lens, collecting information about the practices and preferences of many users. When we can address a question to a large sample of library users, we may be able to generalize about their preferences for programming, services, collections, space, and more. As an instrument, the survey has the advantage that it can help a library collect a large volume of data in a relatively standardized form—data that is ripe for analysis, promising a solid foundation for decision-making. For example, a survey of a specific demographic of library users may help a library to identify the optimal time to schedule an event, like a panel discussion or a children's story hour. A survey of library cardholders active within a particular time frame may inform decision-making about collection or service priorities. Beyond responses to a single question, surveys conducted over time can help librarians to identify trends in user preferences or behavior.

Obversely, surveys can be designed for inclusivity. Rather than surveying a population based on a defined interest, surveys distributed to a sample of a demographic group may elicit responses from infrequent library users, or those who do not go to the library at all. Surveys distributed electronically also give remote users, or patrons who use the library's virtual services more than its physical services, a greater voice than surveys distributed exclusively to people who use the physical space. A random sample of a university student population would include nonusers, online-only users, and students whose library use varies based on their major area of study. Similarly, a public library obtaining a survey panel that includes community members outside its user database can learn about the broader perceptions and needs of these nonlibrary users.

Surveys can help librarians to test the validity of professional observations and anecdotes. For example, library administrators may notice an increasing number of questions about the availability of library spaces for public use. A survey of the library's community or patron population might inform changes to policies or plans for renovation or expansion.

Just as a survey can be used to confirm observations and other forms of feedback, it can also put into context the prevalence of user attitudes and experiences. "Squeaky wheels" may or may not represent the needs or desires of other users. When the resources to respond to user wish lists are limited (as is frequently the case), surveys can help determine which interventions will be most welcome. In our experience, when we asked about the appearance of our university library—a place that several employees had decried as dingy and depressing—we learned that while no one considered the library to be attractive, the interior and exterior appearance simply didn't rate in our users' minds as important or formative of a good library experience, as the few (but vocal) library staff had indicated.

Surveys are a flexible and affordable tool for gathering large quantities of data. Although questionnaires were once expensive and time consuming to administer by mail, phone, or in person, Web-based survey platforms have made surveys more accessible to librarians than ever before. The majority of library users may access surveys through e-mail and text or through library Web sites, social media, or other online promotion. Web-based survey platforms allow library staff to review data in the aggregate, and many fee-based tools even perform some basic, descriptive data analysis. For populations that would be better reached through paper surveys, their responses can be collected and integrated into the digital tool so that they can be analyzed in the aggregate.

The way that librarians use survey data is as important as the information collected and the tools being used. Surveys constitute a powerful tool for evidence-based decision-making and advocacy when they are designed well and validated. Librarians can incorporate survey findings into strategic planning, program development, policymaking, and fundraising. While survey data is not a substitute for circulation data, gate counts, and other methods of analyzing user behavior, survey findings help libraries tell the story of library use and library users, demonstrating their impact and inspiring new directions based on the expressed desires of user groups. Through satisfaction measures, ranking, and self-assessment measures, survey responses can bring the circumstances surrounding usage data into sharp relief. For example, when we asked about format preferences, we knew that our usage data indicated a reasonable use of e-books. Anecdotal evidence from both the reference desk and the Interlibrary Loan (ILL) system revealed at least some resistance and/or confusion related to the format, but it was hard to quantify how much of our user population had strong preferences. As it turned out, over half of our user population stated that they preferred print books only.

WHEN SURVEYS DON'T DELIVER

The popularity of survey questionnaires belies the potential pitfalls of this tool. In practice, surveys often fail to deliver for several reasons. First, the research question may not be matched to the research method. The most common example of this occurs when the survey is designed to capture data that already is collected more accurately via other means, such as: "How often do you check out a book or other items from the library?" Rates of circulation can be extracted from the Integrated Library System (ILS), while the individual user's memory may or may not align with reality. Another example of a mismatch in purpose is a survey designed primarily to generate ideas from users, a task more suited to focus groups, where participants can synergistically develop, elaborate, and refine ideas together. Not all observations require quantitative validation; additional methods, including interviews or usability studies, may be more appropriate.

Second, the method of soliciting participation in a survey may not be matched to the research question or the appropriate population. For example, surveys distributed to active library cardholders are unlikely to receive responses from nonlibrary users, so if a research question relates to declining library use, the researchers also should include people with inactive accounts.

Third, the survey may be too long, be difficult to read, or have other qualities that frustrate the respondents. In addition to following the best practices for user-friendly survey design, the value of considering user input before and after constructing a survey is crucial for success. User testing often can identify jargon or other terminology that is unfamiliar to nonlibrarians. Response options that are confusing or missing are also frequently identified by attentive survey testers.

For those who argue that librarians overuse surveys and that they should use other methods to learn more about their populations (Halpern et al. 2015), the real problem may be that library users are inundated with well-intentioned but ineffective survey instruments. We can reframe our thinking about surveys if we take some time to recognize what the survey is for (and what it is not for), and how it can help us learn more about what library communities do, think, want, and feel.

WHAT'S SO HARD ABOUT DESIGNING SURVEYS?

A well-designed survey can be revelatory. Data showing library users' feelings, behavior, and preferences are invaluable tools for decision-making. Library user preferences are the linchpin of organizational decision-making, and we have many ways to track how patrons actually use our collections, services, and spaces. However, going directly to users and asking questions offers us insights that circulation statistics or gate counts leave unaddressed. Surveys of library users can help librarians to empathize with our communities, to define problems, and to take action.

While surveys help us to collect data that cannot be monitored through other systems, we must remember that survey data is unique because it represents a subset of library user opinions. Data collected from surveys is self-reported, and it accounts for an individual's:

- Attitudes, feelings, and preferences
- Past behavior
- Predictions of future behavior
- Dimensions of personality

By their very nature, survey responses are subjective. Taken together, analysis of a set of survey responses can reveal trends. We conduct surveys not because we are concerned about one patron's opinion, but because the feelings of our collective community of patrons may offer us insights about the present or the future. A single patron might complain about the lack of nutritious options in the library's vending machines; but the full collection of survey responses might reveal the broader point that most patrons are unaware that the vending machines exist at all, underlying a way-finding issue.

SURVEYS ELICIT SELF-REPORTED DATA

When we invite library users to respond to surveys, we build knowledge about our communities and our users' relationships with the library. The self-reported nature of survey data means that we can rely on such instruments to give us only certain kinds of data.

Attitudes, feelings, and preferences:
- Please choose the option that best describes your opinion of interlibrary loan.
- Do you prefer to study alone or in a group?

Accounts of past behavior:
- How many library programs have you attended in the last three months?

Predictions of future behavior:

- What types of spaces would you like to use in a reimagined library?
- How frequently would you like to receive information about the library?

Dimensions of personality:

- When you are spending time in the library, do you prefer spaces where socializing and talking are welcome?

Unfortunately, survey design is easily derailed. Libraries often deploy surveys with unclear themes or objectives. This may happen for organizational reasons. In the haste to get a survey out, some libraries will skip important steps in survey planning, design, and testing.

Common pitfalls of surveys deployed by libraries are excessive length and illogical organization. This often happens when staff members from several units of the library are interested in a hodgepodge of topics, which becomes the framework for a complicated survey instrument. Surveys like this create high-burden interactions (Crawford, Couper, and Lamias 2001, p. 146) for libraries and the people who respond to our surveys. Conventional wisdom states that survey designers should endeavor to reduce the burdens of length and complexity for survey respondents (Dillman, Smyth, and Christian 2014). Research shows that survey respondents find longer surveys irritating; as the respondent's goodwill diminishes, response accuracy also declines. Respondents are more likely to skip questions at the end of longer surveys or leave negative, neutral, or contradictory responses. This kind of behavior is popularly attributed to decision fatigue, a concept in psychology (Vohs et al. 2008) described for general audiences in *The New York Times* by John Tierney (2011). The idea of decision fatigue has been applied widely in user experience and usability studies, as well as in situations like medicine and judicial settings, in which professionals must make a long string of high-stakes decisions.

In future chapters, we discuss how the principles of design thinking can aid in survey development, especially the practice of empathizing with the survey audience. If we try to empathize with library users, we can develop surveys that they are willing to complete. We also discuss the idea that altruism and goodwill may be strong motivations for completing a library's survey. The worst possible outcome in survey design, then, would be a confusing survey that squanders the respondent's warm feelings toward the library.

Long surveys that cover a wide range of subjects also pose a problem for analysis. With a grab bag of results, librarians may have difficulty gauging the significance of one response over another. The solution to this problem is not to put the "most important" questions at the beginning of the survey. Rather, designing a survey that seeks only "important" information is the best approach.

Surveys may be developed in a vacuum, without collaboration, testing, reflection, or revision. Librarians may skip these steps because survey preparation seems to be a relatively simple and straightforward procedure, and also because they are eager to distribute the survey and see the results. In addition to length, hastily deployed surveys often suffer from questions that lack clarity for a general audience. Collaboration offers librarians opportunities to edit survey questions, reflect on whether a question addresses the survey's theme and purpose, and ultimately, revise questions and test them again.

Unfortunately, when surveys do not yield useful results, there is little that one can do except to plan better next time. Do-overs are seldom possible without trying the patience of the respondents. In the best-case scenario, we learn from our mistakes. In the worst—and perhaps most common—case, inconclusive results are used anyway in order to salvage the effort. In either case, however, the data collected can be difficult or impossible to interpret.

Planning a Library Survey

A survey with a clear purpose is more likely to collect useful and usable data. The purpose may seem obvious initially, but taking the time to evaluate assumptions and refine ideas about the survey will improve the research outcomes. The goal is to articulate an essential information need, and then determine how the data gathered will be used for decision-making. Even if the general intent of a survey seems fairly obvious, a plan will help you create a survey that uses the respondent's time well and yields actionable data. Inspired by the concepts of Design Thinking, we suggest that you plan your survey in a structured way that enables you to refine and improve the instrument.

Survey planning should be a collaborative effort. This does not mean that you must involve every employee of your organization in the planning or execution of the survey, but no research instrument should be developed in a vacuum. Large libraries increasingly employ staff members who conduct user experience and assessment research, but most libraries do not have that luxury. Regardless of the size of your library, a group of stakeholders can gather together to brainstorm about gaps in knowledge about the patron experience. To help your library operate, improve, or grow, what do you need to know about your patrons' feelings, attitudes, or behaviors? Once the survey's purpose is defined clearly, the work of drafting a survey prototype can be turned over to a smaller group.

EMPATHIZE WITH YOUR RESPONDENTS

After you have assembled your team, planning the survey should begin with a series of discussions. The intent of the survey may seem fairly

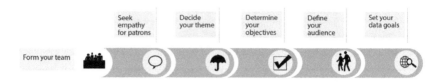

FIGURE 2.1. Planning Your Survey

obvious to everyone involved, but these preliminary discussions can help you avoid the common pitfalls of surveys.

Taking a cue from the practice of Design Thinking, the first survey design discussion should be framed around empathy. From the *Oxford English Dictionary,* the meaning of *empathy* is "the ability to understand and appreciate another person's feelings, experience, etc." In the context of survey design, empathy involves thinking deeply about the user experience, considering questions like the following:

- What information do you lack about the library user experience?
- What do your users want you to know about their experience in the library?

You may begin the design process knowing that you need to conduct a survey about a specific aspect of the library. In that case, your questions will take the same form as given previously, but with slightly more specificity. For example, "What information do you lack about the patron experience with circulation policies?"

Empathy sounds easy enough in a helping profession like librarianship. Unfortunately, some all-too-familiar dispositions may be obstacles to empathy:

- "This is the way we do it."
- "We tried to change that, and it didn't work."
- "If people would just . . ."
- "I know this is complicated, but . . ."

Empathizing with your library community will help you to ask questions that may reveal information that challenges the status quo. Empathy might make you uncomfortable, but remember that surveys are about exploration—asking questions that help us understand and grow. Beginning a survey design process in this way helps us to set aside predispositions and work toward meaningful inquiry. Developing some feelings of empathy for your survey respondents will set the stage for defining the key elements of the survey instrument.

DEFINE THE THEME

Defining a survey's theme will help you evaluate what does and does not belong in the survey and ensure that each part of it functions as part of the whole. Like empathizing, defining the theme of the survey is a broad exercise rather than a granular one, and its purpose is to set the scope of the inquiry. Think of the theme as an umbrella—the questions included in the survey will fit under that umbrella. Examples:

- Building renovation
- Climate of the library for first-generation students
- Scheduling and availability
- Patron satisfaction

Your survey's theme should draw on the thoughts and conclusions gathered during your empathy exercises. It is possible that you will identify more than one major theme for a given survey. But before you combine themes within a single survey, consider how they will work together. Maintaining a coherent logic to your survey reduces the burden of the survey response, helping your respondents remain engaged and committed to completing the survey. When looking at multiple themes for inclusion, consider the following questions:

- Do the themes pair well together, or do they address disparate parts of the library experience?
- What effect will addressing both themes have on the survey's length and usability?
- Have you considered running more than one survey in the near future? Could you split your themes into multiple surveys?
- Would addressing multiple themes be effective, or merely convenient?

DEFINE THE OBJECTIVES

Once the survey team has defined a theme, the group can begin to brainstorm what they hope to learn from the library community. Objectives of surveys vary widely, ranging from forward-thinking surveys designed to help plan services or facilities, to more reflective assessments of patron satisfaction. In any case, the survey's objective should be articulated in a simple, easily understood statement or statements, like the following:

- We want to learn how users experience the library.
- We want to learn what library users value.
- We want to learn how the library is perceived.
- We want to learn what's missing from our services.
- We want to learn what our users hope we will do.

By defining your objectives, you are laying the groundwork for effective question design. Identifying what you want to know allows you to test the value of the questions that you generate against your stated objectives.

SAMPLE THEME: ADULT SUMMER PROGRAMMING SCHEDULE

Sample objectives:

- We want to learn why users participated or didn't participate last summer.
- We want to learn what barriers prevented users from attending events.
- We want to learn about favorite events or topics.
- We want to learn what would bring people back for another program.

DEFINE THE AUDIENCE

Surveys are powerful instruments for gathering information from large populations. However, it is rarely the case that a *census*, or response from the entire library community, is necessary to produce meaningful data. As you brainstorm about information needs, you may notice that population characteristics emerge. You may have questions that address a specific population or need:

- "How are nontraditional students [age 24+] using the library?"
- "What services do patrons whose first language isn't English desire?"
- "How do library fines affect the perception of the library?"

Your survey may be relevant to your entire patron community or only to a subset. Because many online survey platforms allow you to select questions to be shown to specific subsets of your audience, it is possible to write an online survey with questions for both broad and specific audiences:

Display this question if Yes is selected for:

Have you been fined for late or missing material in the last 12 months?

When you were fined, which statement most accurately reflects your actions?

○ I paid my fine in full and continued to use the library.

○ I paid my fine in full but avoided the library.

○ I paid part of my fine so that I could continue to use the library.

○ I did not pay my fine and have avoided the library.

We strongly recommend this approach; however, if you choose to go this route, you must write every question with a target population in mind. In a well-designed survey, your design should feature questions that a substantial portion of the target population of survey respondents could answer truthfully. There is no standard rule of thumb, but we suggest that you ask yourself, "Is this survey relevant to at least 20 percent of my target population?" Further, 100 percent of the questions included in a survey should be understandable to the target population, meaning that questions should be rigorously tested for clarity, and to eliminate the jargon that is so common to the library profession.

Whether a survey audience is general or specific, the planning stage is an important time to consider the needs of survey respondents. For example, the instrument should be translated if the survey audience includes library users who primarily speak languages other than English. If your library already produces material in languages other than English, it may be easy to determine which languages to select. Data from the U.S. Census can help you to identify community characteristics that will influence your survey's language or other features. Accessibility is also a crucial consideration, whether a survey is distributed electronically or on paper. While Web-based surveys are likely the most convenient way for any library to distribute a survey, planning to ensure that the Web-based instrument can be interpreted with a screen reader will help respondents who are blind or visually impaired.

DEFINE WHAT KIND OF DATA—AND ANTICIPATE HOW YOU WILL USE IT

After settling on a theme, or a set of related themes, your next step is to decide what kind of data could help you to answer questions on that theme or themes. From a strategic standpoint, the theme or themes will help you decide whether the survey is the appropriate tool to meet your information need. As you consider the information need, a key issue is that survey data is largely self-reported information about individual feelings, thoughts, perceptions, and experiences. When you're designing a survey, you want to stay focused on data that will show you something that only individuals can tell you. The themes listed in this chapter all represent information needs that can be addressed with survey responses.

Ultimately, you and your colleagues may conclude that your survey data will join a constellation of data points that contribute to decision-making. For example, a library planning a renovation or expansion could examine historic program attendance data in combination with a survey that asks the community residents what kinds of programming or events they would like to attend at the library. If you conclude that your survey's theme can be served by self-reported data, you will be able to move on to developing survey questions. As you write each question, consider what your organization will do with the data collected by this question. Scenarios for survey data use in decision-making include the following:

- Gauging the popularity of a service, a collection, or a proposal for change. The results of a survey may show staff, administrators, or both where time and money is best allocated.
- Identifying patron preferences or wishes for specific hardware or software available in the library, in order to justify equipment expenditures, or changes to equipment provided by the library.
- Capturing the opinions and needs of a specific user demographic to provide evidence that funding is needed for a specific program or service. For example, a library may be writing a grant proposal for

expanded services for children and youth, and the results of a survey of area teachers can help you to articulate what an important constituency would value most in a new position.

- Collecting satisfaction data at regular intervals to establish benchmarks of quality or to report to administrators, municipal agencies, funders, or accrediting bodies.

Because surveys sound easy to put together, libraries and librarians often deploy them "just to see what we learn." While this approach may yield an insight or two, a well-articulated intention helps survey teams to design useful surveys that collect meaningful results without excessively burdening the respondents.

TIMES WHEN A SURVEY IS NOT THE RIGHT APPROACH

- You are interested in asking many open-ended questions in order to gather unique individual perspectives. Focus groups or interviews are likely a better option.
- You want to demonstrate that the library caused a definitive change. Self-reported data from surveys cannot establish causation.
- You want to evaluate patron learning. Because surveys can only collect self-reported data, evidence of learning is difficult for the respondent to provide, and impossible for you to analyze.
- You plan to cherry pick the data to affirm preexisting views.
- You do not plan to use the data for decision making, communication, or another defined purpose.

If early discussions lead to the conclusion that a survey will not serve the library's information needs, the team can discuss other methods of collecting meaningful information from users. These methods may include examination of previous research by your own library or other libraries; consideration of formal input from the community gathered by other entities (e.g., a local government, a school district office, or a college/university's office of institutional research); or new investigations involving nonsurvey research methods, like focus groups. Your plan for using the survey data may be to analyze it and report the results publicly or internally. Alternatively, you may be collecting the data to help you make a single decision. You may be planning to write an article in a trade or scholarly publication, for instance. In any of these cases, a survey is an instrument that collects a particular type of user data. If you conclude that this data will tell you something you need to know, the survey is right for you.

3

Survey Methods That Work for Libraries

99% of library surveys primarily reveal that libraries love giving surveys.

—Fake Library Statistics, Twitter *(2012)*

Surveys are versatile tools that enable researchers to collect data from well-defined populations. While libraries have long conducted patron surveys, the relative ease of building and distributing online surveys has inspired more librarians to seek patron opinions with survey instruments. There is no doubt that surveys can collect information useful for decision-making, but surveys are often designed hastily and without proper testing, or they collect information that is difficult to analyze. Considering survey methods can help you make choices that make your survey more useful to your library. While the methods of survey research are not instinctive, it is important to remember that the survey is an instrument with strong methodological underpinnings (Connaway and Radford 2017). In this chapter, we discuss some key considerations in survey research that will help you to collect significant results.

WHAT DO WE MEAN WHEN WE SAY "SURVEY"?

There are many types of surveys, but this book focuses on instruments in the broad category of "descriptive surveys." Descriptive surveys help libraries to develop quantifiable profiles of a library community—its characteristics, opinions, and behavior. These tools enable a population to respond to a set of questions in order to collect (mostly) quantitative data. Descriptive surveys can illuminate several types of information: frequency of a particular activity, characteristics of a so-called typical respondent, comparison between two or more groups, and relationships among variables. Here is an example of a descriptive survey question:

> Thinking about the last time you entered the library's downtown location, were you:
>
> - By yourself
> - With another adult
> - With a minor child (under the age of 18)
> - With an adult/child combination

Descriptive surveys are common across all sectors of the economy, and we observe that libraries use this kind of tool heavily. Descriptive surveys may capture a population's opinion at a point in time, and they can capture trend data if administered over a period of time or at specific intervals. The reliability of survey data depends on the methods used to collect the data. This is not a social science textbook, but we recommend that librarians developing surveys make intentional choices about their research methods.

QUANTITATIVE VERSUS QUALITATIVE: WHAT KIND OF INFORMATION DO I NEED IN ORDER TO MAKE A DECISION?

Surveys can collect a mix of quantitative and qualitative data, but most survey questions are designed so that the answers can be easily quantified so that descriptive statistical results can be presented. Surveys are not an appropriate method for all research questions. If you are asking a question that can be answered numerically with averages, proportions, and rates, then a well-designed survey will work for you. If your research question is experiential, a survey may not aid your inquiry. Some librarians have argued that our profession relies too heavily on the survey and that we should explore qualitative methods like focus groups, interviews, observational studies, rubrics, and other tools (Halpern et al. 2015). We agree, but we believe that because most practicing library workers lack training in research methods, the problem is that information professionals must learn to design surveys well in order to determine whether this method is right for any research.

If you are not comfortable with statistical methods, do not fear phrases like "quantitative," "qualitative," or "descriptive statistics." Even if you have not taken a statistics course, you are certainly able to conduct a survey and extract descriptive statistics from the results. Here is an example of a survey question that yields a descriptive result:

If the library opened one additional evening a week, which evening would you prefer?

- Tuesday
- Wednesday
- Thursday

Results:
53 percent of respondents prefer Tuesday evenings.
43 percent of respondents prefer Wednesday evenings.

Quantitative data is not more valuable than qualitative data per se, but analyzing qualitative data creates more work. Depending on the research method, qualitative data can emerge from text, recordings, or images. In the case of surveys, qualitative data comes from open-ended comment fields, but nonsurvey research methods like focus groups, interviews, and observational studies could produce other kinds of qualitative data not discussed here. Survey comments must be coded in order to become "data" that can be analyzed (see Chapter 9). The qualitative data usually comes from a few short- or long-answer text boxes in which respondents can share additional thoughts, express narrative opinions, or explain an "Other" answer. For example, a 10-question survey with various multiple-choice format questions may conclude with an open-ended question soliciting additional thoughts, like this one:

Would you like to share any other thoughts about your experience using the library?

As librarians, we know that every patron has a unique story and relationship with the library, and we strive to respect individual identities and experiences. As a result, we may be particularly inclined to include ample opportunity for people to share their thoughts "in their own words." While we do not argue that librarians should avoid or eliminate open-ended questions from surveys, we urge caution when using them. Qualitative information collected in surveys must be coded for the data to have any conclusive meaning. Therefore, quantitative data is analyzed more readily, lending itself to speedier decision-making.

Qualitative data feels more meaningful (even personal) than quantitative data because it gives the survey respondent the opportunity to praise a service, a collection, or even a library employee or program. These comments may feel like a feather in your cap. Similarly, patrons often use open-ended questions to express negative feelings, which may be interpreted as insulting or nonconstructive, or else as issues that require an urgent response. It is hard not to give more weight to emphatic comments, either positive or negative. Strong negative comments often draw our attention to a problem that may not be viewed as such by the rest of the survey population. When qualitative responses are optional, it is important to note the total number of nonresponses, as well as the written comments, to help you put the data in context.

Survey research is not about the individual response; it is about the aggregate. In our own library, we asked patrons if they had any additional thoughts about the library's environment. Some respondents commented bitterly about the temperature in the building; however, coding revealed that the total number of responses about temperature was less than 3 percent of all comments. Qualitative results can be analyzed accurately only if they are coded. Coding open-ended comments can be a revelatory process, but it is laborious and often reveals only statistically insignificant data points. Therefore, we strongly recommend that you limit the number of survey questions that include open-ended responses. Consider whether you will have the time to code the data properly to analyze the results, and whether you will be able to act on your analysis. If your survey research team is inclined to develop a questionnaire with many open-ended comment fields, we suggest that the team revisit whether surveying is the best research method for your question. Other methods, including focus groups, interviews, and observational studies, may be more appropriate.

SAMPLING: WHO AND HOW MANY WILL YOU SURVEY?

By design, surveys do not collect data from 100 percent of a population. Indeed, most survey administrators send their survey to a sample of the total population that could respond to the questions. Survey respondents are often referred to as a "panel." With an adequate sample size and response rate, the panel's responses can usually be interpreted as generalizable.

Determining a sample size is tricky, and we suspect that most librarians who conduct surveys just hope to get enough responses. When planning a survey, we recommend that you work backward from your survey objective to identify the target audience, as discussed in Chapter 2. Who among your users and nonusers can address your survey objective? You may determine that anyone could respond to your questions; more likely, however, you will identify a subset of the library community:

- Example: A large law firm's library identifies all junior associates for a survey about the instruction and training that they desire.
- Example: A state historical society identifies all recent individual donors for a survey about plans for expansion.
- Example: A school district identifies teachers of grades 6–9 as the population to survey about the need for a new collection or resource.
- Example: A public library identifies patrons who have not used the library for more than 12 months as the population to survey about satisfaction or unmet needs.
- Example: A college library identifies nontraditional students as the population to survey about how they use the library.

How many responses will you need in order to answer your question?

Once you've determined the target population of your survey, you must decide how large your panel must be to obtain meaningful results. You have choices about how to determine the size of the population that you will invite to participate. One option is a "census," which means that every member of a group would receive a survey. Generally, a census is inappropriate for survey research except when the target population is small and well defined (e.g., all parents of minors who hold cards at a public library, all nurses who use a hospital's information center, or all first-year students enrolled at a university). More likely, you will distribute your survey to a representative sample of the target population. In survey research methods, this is called "probability sampling." Whether a census or a probability sample, never assume that every person invited to take the survey will respond. Nonetheless, survey results are more easily analyzed and produce more generalizable responses when they are received from a greater percentage of those invited.

Some people question why a census is not more representative (not to mention democratic) than sending a survey to a random sample of that population. A census is a reasonable approach in the case of a limited population. For example, a school librarian would be wise to send an annual teacher survey to 100 percent of the teachers in a school. Even if the

Library population: ✦ ✦ ✦ ✦ ✦ ✦ ✦ ✦ ✦
Census sample: ✦ ✦ ✦ ✦ ✦ ✦ ✦ ✦ ✦
Random sample: ✦ ✦ ✦ ✦ ✦
Narrow population: ✦ ✦ ✦

FIGURE 3.1. Populations and Samples

school is large, the population of teachers is well defined and uniform in its association with, and access to, the library's services. For large populations, or communities with diverse experiences and expectations of a library, census surveys present several problems. For instance, social scientists who research survey methods have found that they do not decrease or minimize bias. A census survey is also impractical for libraries with large or dispersed populations, and libraries that send surveys at regular intervals risk creating "survey fatigue" in their user communities if they send everyone a survey on a regular basis.

So how do you calculate the size of a random sample? Several research methods textbooks listed in Appendix G offer extensive instructions for calculating a sample size. You can also use a sample-size calculator, such as the one provided on the Web site of Creative Research Systems (https://www.surveysystem.com/sscalc.htm). A sample-size calculator will ask you to enter the following numbers to obtain an accurate sample size:

> **Confidence level:** This reflects your confidence that the respondents would repeat the same answer if they received the survey a second time. Generally, 95 percent is a conventional confidence level.
>
> **Confidence interval**: A 4-point interval is conventional. This means that you accept a margin of error of 4 percentage points.
>
> **Population size**: This references the size of the total population for whom the survey is relevant.

Sample size calculators will ask you to enter your data into a form in order to calculate the sample size that you need to have valid, generalizable data.

Confidence level	95%	95%	95%
Confidence interval	4	4	4
Population size	10,000 enrolled students	60,000 city residents	25,000 cardholders
This will produce:			
Sample size	567	595	587

Having calculated the appropriate sample size, you know how many responses you need. To calculate how many people should be invited to respond to the survey, you must project a response rate. If you predict that 10% of recipients will respond, then your sample size should equal 10% of total invited to take the survey. For example:

Sample size	567	595	587
10%	5,670	5,950	5,870

Projecting your response rate is tricky. Naturally, you hope that the majority of survey recipients will enthusiastically join your survey panel, but even the library's most faithful users may defy expectations when it comes to taking surveys. If you have previously surveyed a population with the same profile, project your response rate based on that data. However, if you have not surveyed a population, be conservative and predict a low response rate. For future surveys, you will have a more accurate benchmark.

Oversampling

Some populations are more difficult to reach with surveys. This may be because some demographics are less likely to respond to survey invitations in general, are suspicious or fearful of the consequences of participation, or belong to groups historically excluded from survey research. To ensure representation by such a group, libraries can consider distributing a survey to larger samples of a particular demographic.

Participant Recruitment, Incentives, and Nonresponse Bias

In Chapter 8, we discuss the mechanisms and modes of survey distribution. Sample size and response rate are important, and so is the strategy used to recruit survey respondents. Recruiting survey participants may sound as easy as dipping into patron contact data, but social scientists have documented a general decline in survey participation since the early 1990s. With some notable exceptions, most survey participants are "self-selecting"—that is, they choose to participate. When you think about recruiting survey respondents, focus on what will motivate library users to make the choice to start—and complete—your survey. Noted social scientist and survey researcher Eleanor Singer identified some general categories of survey participant motivation in *The Palgrave Handbook of Survey Research* (Singer 2018):

- Altruism
- Egoistic reasons, which may include compensation, a desire to learn something new, or even that the participant enjoys taking surveys
- Reputation of the surveying organization
- Topic of the survey

Library users are likely motivated by a mix of factors when they choose to respond to a survey. For active users of the library, participation may be inspired by goodwill for the library and its mission, or a desire to do something good for an organization that they value. However, responses from infrequent library users or nonusers can be more difficult to obtain, and these responses will enrich data about most aspects of the library's work. Depending on a library's resources, a variety of incentive models may help recruit a diverse array of participants. Online survey participants are often offered the opportunity to enter a lottery. At our own library, we have offered respondents the chance to win one of four gift cards to a major online retailer. Libraries could also offer in-kind services. A lottery for in-kind services may be more financially realistic for most libraries, especially if the library frequently deploys surveys. Respondents could enter to win any of the following:

- Access to the library's meeting, event, or study space
- A personalized story hour
- Advance copies of books that the library may have received from publishers
- Homemade crafts or baked goods donated by a "friends of the library" group
- One-on-one instructional session about a library resource, like genealogy tools or a three-dimensional printer

Rather than lotteries, compensation for survey participation may include a monetary incentive. Monetary incentives are extremely common in surveys deployed by large commercial survey organizations, like Gallup. The body of research about their effect shows that monetary incentives, particularly prepaid incentives, are generally more effective than gifts of tangible items (Singer 2018, 406). However, there is no research-based guideline about how little or how much money motivates participation. Most libraries do not have the resources to compensate every respondent, so we encourage librarians to consider their available resources and think creatively about sustainable incentives that will encourage a user community to participate.

RESEARCH ETHICS

Bearing in mind that survey participation is voluntary and that participants have self-selected, ethical considerations are critical. Libraries must avoid coercion or undue influence when planning a survey incentive. For example, a librarian teaching an information literacy class at a high school or college should not make course grades contingent on participation in a survey. Similarly, library privileges should not be revoked or compromised if a person declines to respond to the survey. In addition, calls for survey participation should not be aggressive. An initial invitation and one or two reminders to take a survey are sufficient; additional requests for participation may be viewed as harassment.

NONRESPONSE BIAS

A major reason to offer survey incentives is to attract respondents who would not ordinarily be interested in taking a survey. Within the field of survey research, there is substantial concern about "nonresponse bias." This phenomenon can emerge in any form of survey research. The survey data can be biased or misleading if conclusions are drawn from a nonrepresentative population. In contrast to self-selected participants, people who do not respond to surveys may actively self-*deselect;* that is, they had an opportunity to take the survey but chose not to participate. During the 2016 presidential election season, for instance, most public opinion polls did not project that Donald Trump would win the race. For example, the *Washington Post/ABC News* tracking poll projected that Hillary Clinton would win the election by 3 percentage points (Langer et al. 2016). In postelection analysis, many people hypothesized that nonresponse bias was to blame for inaccurate projections. The Pew Research Center says that nonresponse bias "occurs when certain kinds of people systematically do not respond to surveys despite equal opportunity outreach to all parts of the electorate" (Mercer, Deane, and McGeeney 2016). This definition applies to any population of potential survey respondents. Some people simply will not respond for a wide variety of personal reasons.

The idea of nonresponse bias sounds theoretical, and of course, the stakes of most library surveys are unlikely to rise to the level of a presidential election. But a library also must deal with nonresponse bias when trying to reach people who are not library users, those whose use of the library has declined, or people who face structural barriers to the using the survey instrument. For libraries, oversampling may address this problem by amplifying the opportunity that some demographics have to take a survey. Oversampling may ameliorate nonresponse bias, but it is difficult to control for. However, we can take a simple lesson from the political example—generally, the larger and more diverse your respondent pool, the more reliable the results. Unfortunately, there is little evidence that incentives improve diversity of survey respondents (Singer 2018, 411–412), which does not help any survey researcher to address the problem of nonresponse bias. Some survey researchers argue that improving the survey instrument itself is a more effective way to improve the outcome.

TIMING

The timing of your survey is determined by your survey objective: one-time, trend, or longitudinal, and ongoing surveys all have advantages, depending on the theme and objectives determined by your survey design team. The timing of a survey instrument should be determined by the research question. Many research questions have a shelf-life, and the data collected will be useful only once. Some questions are perennial, though, and when asked over and over again, the aggregate answers may point to important trends.

One-Time

A one-time survey captures the opinion of users at a single point in time. The researchers may not intend, at least initially, to repeat the survey at regular intervals. If they do repeat the survey, questions may be altered or adjusted in the next iteration. Nonetheless, one-time surveys have an important place in gauging library user interest in programs, services, collections, and spaces. These surveys may help the library to chart future directions or to make a decision. One-time surveys often revolve around specific themes or questions: parking and transportation; fines; library hours; desire for materials, content, and formats; or other point-in-time issues.

Trend Surveys

The longitudinal survey (also known as a "trend" survey) is an instrument that is administered at regular intervals over time. Surveys about satisfaction with aspects of library experience are a typical example of longitudinal instruments. Each time that it is administered, the respondents receive the same questions. Classic longitudinal surveys are conducted with cohorts of participants, which means that the researchers return to the same group of participants at regular intervals to track progress or change. Most libraries probably lack the resources to conduct a classic longitudinal survey, but assembling a cohort of respondents is typically unnecessary for most library inquiries anyway. A notable longitudinal survey employed by many academic libraries is LibQUAL+, which allows libraries to benchmark user satisfaction over time. The sample of respondents represents the same profile of library user, but the same individuals are not necessarily included in every sample. The assumption with this survey is that improvements or declines in patron opinion reflect library performance.

Trend surveys also can be used to collect feedback from users continuously, similar to a comment box. Data collected from user feedback forms could be analyzed quarterly, annually, or other intervals to benchmark trends in patron feelings and satisfaction levels.

4

Scopes of Experience

The burning question has always been: How is this brand signifi-cant in the lives of its users?

—Cynthia Round *(Steimer 2018)*

INTRODUCTION

The brand that Cynthia Round is referring to here is the Metropolitan Museum of Art. In 2016, she led a successful rebranding that focused on the relationship between the museum and its users. There is a tendency in library surveys to focus on either future plans or those things that we spend a lot of money on: building renovations, programming, collections. As library staff, you have a good idea of what you want to ask your users. But to fully maximize the effort of both survey-writers and survey-takers, it is best to think not just in terms of your immediate survey objectives, but also your user's experiences. Paraphrasing Cynthia Round, how is the library significant in the lives of its users? The kind of information that you can get by asking about the context of your most salient questions will help in interpreting the answers. The time that you spend cultivating empathy for your users will help you to frame questions that respondents will be able to answer based on their own experiences. For example, when designing a survey to determine user satisfaction with your e-book options, questions about platforms and devices, amount of time spent reading, features, and troubleshooting can be used to illuminate the preferences of casual browsers versus power-readers.

In order to think about the context of your survey objectives, it is useful to look at the scopes of experience that represent the potential points of connection between your users and the library. LibQUAL+, a survey of service quality widely used by academic libraries, explores three dimensions of library performance—"Effect of Service, Information Control, and Library as Place." While we do not discourage libraries from exploring standardized survey tools—indeed, our own library has administered LibQUAL+—our experience is that libraries of all kinds collect survey data for major and minor reasons. The questions that library users are most likely to be able to address accurately emerge from four scopes of user experience—service, space, communication, and collections. No survey must include all four scopes of user experience. Sometimes these scopes overlap, but they are a useful framework for thinking through what to ask your users. It is worth noting that librarians also conduct surveys in other domains. For example, human resources (HR) units survey staff about employment experiences, and librarians often survey each other about professional practices, education, training, and other needs. The guidelines articulated in this book apply to both those scenarios.

Surveys are a way at getting at the user experience, but only if they are constructed to allow respondents to describe their genuine feelings. Aaron Schmidt and Amanda Etches (2014) describe user experience as "how someone feels when using a product or service." If the survey is a product, we have to think outside our own roles as service providers when developing the product. As Schmidt and Etches note, librarians are not the same as our users. We must make extra affordances to represent the scopes of experience in a way that reflects the options that our users might select, and not what we *hope* they will select. We do this in the generative phase of identifying experiences within the scopes and designing survey questions, as well as in the user testing and revision process.

Each of the four scopes contains a multitude of possible experiences, states of satisfaction or dissatisfaction, and feelings. The goal in thinking through the scopes relevant to your objectives is not to ask about everything, but to make sure that you are considering all the moving parts related to your survey objective.

COMMUNICATION

Because communication is often our users' entreé into all the other scopes of library experience—the way that they learn about services and collections and the way that they navigate our space—it is an important but often overlooked scope. Not every survey objective is explicitly about communication, but it is a component of many. And more libraries are devoting time to marketing, which the American Marketing Association (2018) defines as "the activity, set of institutions, and processes for creating, communicating, delivering, and exchanging offerings that have value for customers, clients, partners, and society at large." Libraries that strive to market more effectively to their current and potential users can use surveys to understand not only how users view their offerings, but also their various messages.

Communication can include the content that library staff produce on a regular basis, such as guides, reader advisories, Web sites, and social media posts, but it also contains more durable messages, such as library policies, signage and wayfinding, and automated circulation e-mails. The creation of advertisements, news media releases, and public announcements often require a great deal of planning, including thinking about the intended audiences. Surveys are one way to check in on the reach and effectiveness of these communications. Finally, there are the more ephemeral but still important verbal exchanges: conversations at service points, questions from users, and staff remarks.

Web sites	User testing and usage data are commonly used to evaluate library Web sites. With surveys, you can augment this research by focusing on the user's outlook: • Preferences • Perceptions of use • Wishes
Social media	Usage statistics provided by social media sites provide immediate and ongoing snapshots of engagement, but surveys can help fill in the blanks: • Nonlibrary social media participation, which sites, and how much • Preferences
Guides and advisories	While online educational materials come with usage data, the use of paper guides is limited to consumption data. Possible points of interest include: • Gaps in topics/coverage • Satisfaction levels • Points of need

Policies	Occasionally, libraries seek public input as they consider revising or implementing new policies, and surveys can be one way to gather this information. Libraries may ask questions about the ways their policies are communicated: • Accessibility of policy information • User knowledge of key policies
Signage and wayfinding	Signage and wayfinding are usually better examined via user studies, but it is possible to get some limited information from a survey: • Preferences • Satisfaction levels
Automated e-mails	Automated e-mails are a frequent way that libraries communicate with users who borrow materials or use online services, and yet they often go unexamined after they are initially set up. Common topics include: • Preferences • Clarity • Satisfaction levels
Advertising	While there is some data to be analyzed for online ads, surveys are a good way of analyzing the effectiveness of both online and print advertising: • Ads seen by users • Preferences
News and press releases	When libraries work to get in the news or to disseminate important information about the library, it's good to know who is reached: • Which news or government agencies reach library users? • Which stories about the library attract the most attention from users?

SERVICES

Services are the well-established subject of surveys issued by doctor's offices, auto dealers, restaurants, and more. Librarians can use survey data about individual service points or services in general, if it is relevant to their survey objectives. Because services are often a large part of how the user perceives the library, it makes sense that they frequently are featured in library surveys.

We most often think about satisfaction when we think of services, but that is not the only state that users can describe when responding to questions about service. We can find out about respondents' frequency of use and likelihood of future use. We also can ask for characterization about the service experience—was it professional, inclusive, or friendly? Did our users feel valued? Would they recommend the library service to a friend? Asking about every facet of the service experience is neither necessary, feasible, nor wise. Consider which elements will both help you understand your users' experiences and effect changes to improve your service as necessary.

Circulation	Users often can interact with circulation workers at both the beginning and ending of their visit to the library, as well as online and on the phone, and they can answer questions about the following: • Impressions of friendliness and helpfulness • Satisfaction levels • Assistance with reservations of rooms and equipment • Disclosure of checkout policies/periods
Reference	Whether users receive reference assistance from a combined service point or a separate reference desk, specific and general satisfaction questions can be asked about the following: • Satisfaction levels • Impressions of friendliness and helpfulness • Reliability and knowledge of staff • Resolution of reference interviews
Children/ youth services	Questions about services for children or youth often relate to other areas, such as space and collections. Those that are focused on services often involve programming and can be asked after a specific children's program, or more broadly about children's programming in general: • Engagement with children • Convenience of programming scheduling • Program topic preferences • Satisfaction levels
Instruction	Typically, we use surveys to assess instruction at the time that it takes place, but it also can be useful to ask broader questions at various points in time, including: • Frequency or amount of library instruction • Topics or skills that a user would like to learn in the future • Satisfaction levels

Events	As done after instruction, librarians deploy short surveys after library events, but you also can ask about events in general: • Demographics of attendees • Frequency of participation • Future programming desires • Satisfaction levels
Interlibrary Loan (ILL)	Questions about ILL services tend to focus on satisfaction levels with turnaround time, notification, and other elements
Technology assistance Makerspace support Genealogy support	Many libraries have even more specialized areas of support, such as a technology help desk or a makerspace (a do-it-yourself creative space). Assistance with genealogy, career resources, ELL materials, and other more specialized collections also may be important to ask users about the following: • Impressions of friendliness and helpfulness • Knowledge of specialty area • Satisfaction levels

SPACE

It's most typical to ask users about the library as a space when building or remodeling projects are being planned, but it can be useful to get user impressions at other times as well. Asking users about the library environment and facilities can help you prioritize updates to furniture, technology, and other features of the library. And sometimes you may discover, as we did, that problems that you and your staff identify are really not important to your users.

Comfort	Comfort can involve multiple features of the library space, including furnishings, lighting, and temperature: • Satisfaction levels • User feelings
Aesthetics	Questions about appearance and décor can be paired with questions ranking the importance of aesthetic concerns: • Importance level • User feelings

Accessibility	Questions about accessibility are appropriate in relation to many library spaces and services, but a general question about what barriers exist in your library that hinder users with disabilities also can be useful. If you are unsure about the disability demographics of your users, you can include an optional question asking users to identify their type of disability: • Disabilities of users • Type and frequency of access issues
Computing/ Wi-Fi infrastructure	While there are other ways to collect data on the use of Wi-Fi, Internet, computers, and other devices, you can use survey questions to ask users about how they feel about the technology provided: • Preferences • Satisfaction levels
Reading/ study spaces Meeting spaces	Some libraries may already collect data on the use of reading rooms, study spaces, and meeting spaces: • Demographics of use • Satisfaction levels • Awareness of availability, policies
Service points	In addition to asking users about their experiences with actual services, you can ask questions about service points as spaces: • Visibility, clarity of purpose • Accessibility

COLLECTIONS

While much collection assessment is accomplished by looking at circulation and ILL statistics, as well as comparing libraries, it still can be productive to survey users to get an idea about how they feel about the existing collection and their hopes for growth and change.

Physical collections	• Meet needs
Digital collections	• Meet needs • Accessible and usable
Specific collections	• Likely to meet future needs • Predictions of use

Collection format	• Preferences
	• Satisfaction levels
Allocation of resources	• Transparency

Building a survey around the scopes of experience will help it to answer the question with which we began this chapter: How is the library significant in the lives of its users? The scopes are intended to be generative and to encourage reflection on the relationship between the user and the library. But like any framework, they should not be considered as setting absolute limits, particularly for surveys about the intersection of libraries and other aspects of communities.

5

Writing Survey Questions

"Didn't I just answer that question?"
"What do they mean by 'circulation'?"
"How long is this survey, anyway?"

The last thing we want to do to our users is confuse them with our questions. Survey-takers who run into obstacles often quit before they finish, and if they don't, their frustration can color their responses. Questions that seem duplicative, use jargon, and are missing options can confound users. Similarly, the formatting or order of questions can pose problems for users. Writing and ordering questions are important aspects of survey design and ideally should be done in a process that includes drafting, revising, and testing. In this chapter, we will follow a typical workflow for drafting a survey questionnaire, considering how wording, format, and order can optimize the user experience.

DRAFTING A QUESTIONNAIRE

Steps

1. Determine question topics based on survey objectives.
2. Determine question types and draft questions.
3. Determine the order of questions.
4. Perform internal testing and revision.
5. Perform external testing and revision.

Determine Question Topics Based on Survey Objectives

At this point, you've drafted your objectives and considered what scopes of user experience that you want to know more about; now, it is time to get more specific. Most questions touch upon what users do, think, want, or feel. Considering these user actions can help you formulate question topics based on your objectives. Let's consider a survey in which one of the objectives is to get feedback about the library Web site. We know that we can get a lot of information about what users do and think as they use the Web site by analyzing usage data and observing users, but in this scenario, we want to learn about users' outlook and preferences related to the Web site as a source of library information.

Do, Think, Want, Feel

With these parameters defined, we can start brainstorming specific topics. The goal here is to generate possibilities: you're not going to use them all.

Do: Do our users go to our Web site for event information? Do they go to the Web site for policies? Do they go to our Web site for recommendations? To find out about new items? What do users do if they can't find what they're looking for?

Think: Do users prefer to get library information from the Web site? How difficult is it to find what they are looking for?

Want: What information do our users wish they could find on our Web site?

Feel: How do our users feel when they use the Web site?

Once you've brainstormed question topics, you want to step back and determine which of your question topics are worth developing. Your users' attention and goodwill are finite resources. Screening your question topics with the following criteria will help eliminate the ones that will add little or no value to your survey.

Will the Question Be Answerable?

Users can have difficulty answering questions truthfully for a variety of reasons. One reason is that questions can be posed in such a way that there is really only one logical answer. For example, a survey could inquire about whether patrons would like the library to build a café on the ground floor. Regardless of the respondent's likelihood of patronizing the café, the hypothetical answer to such a question is, "Sure! Sounds good!" Questions that rely heavily on the respondent's memory are also unreliable. For example, users may not remember or be able to estimate the number of times that they have visited the library if the period referenced goes too far into the past. For certain types of questions, users may not be good self-reporters if they feel that there is virtue or shame in answering a certain way. For example, respondents are likely to underestimate the amount of time they spend watching television, overestimate how many books they read in a year, or to overstate the likelihood that they would participate in programming about healthy eating.

Can We Act on the Results of the Question?

Curiosity is an insufficient reason to ask any survey question. For example, your survey might open with a question like, "What Jane Austen character are you?" This question seems fun, but beyond a social media meme, what can your library achieve with the answer to this question? If you have no intention of acting on or using the results of a question, either to share them with stakeholders or to inform a future decision, then it's best not to ask it. For one thing, questions that are likely to elicit negative satisfaction responses are also likely to plant the idea that you intend to work to improve satisfaction in that area. If you don't plan to or aren't able to remediate the problem made evident by your survey, it creates the impression that your desire for feedback is pro forma rather than proactive. Similarly, asking about services, products, or projects that are not in the library's future raises expectations that they might be upcoming (and hence create possible disappointment). It also can be demoralizing to create data points that add to the work of interpreting the survey but that you can't act upon.

CURIOSITY AND YOUR SURVEY

For almost every survey we've written, we've had to throw out questions that we asked just because we were curious. These generally get nixed when we ask, "Can we act on the results?" But there are questions that offer results that you don't plan to act on, but that can inform your interpretation of other, more *actionable* questions. A good example would be demographic questions, but there are others.

Do You Already Know the Answer?

The only reason to ask your users a question with a predicable answer is that you need the data to persuade a doubtful partner: an administrator, a funding source, or members of the voting public. For example, in our own library, we have struggled to convince administrators that our university's food service contractor should install a café in the library. While we have ample anecdotal evidence that there is demand for this service, we included the following question on our regular survey of patron satisfaction: "How often does the availability of food or beverage affect where you choose to spend time on campus?"

Determine Question Types and Draft Questions

Survey questions can be grouped into two main categories: open-ended, where your users write their responses by hand; and closed-ended, where you provide fixed options that they choose.

Closed-ended:
What kind of books do you prefer?
○ Print   ○ E-book   ○ Either   ○ It depends

Open-ended:
If you answered, "It depends," why do you say this?

Open-ended questions require more interpretive work—they are expressed in the vernacular of your users and may provide many thoughts in one compounded answer. Usually, you'll want to code open-ended responses or simplify them somehow, so that you can compare and tally your users' written sentiments. This also helps manage the tendency to ascribe more weight to single comments than they deserve in the context of the entire survey. As a result, the majority of your questions on surveys longer than four or five questions should be closed-ended. But there is also the hybrid closed-ended question with the fill-in "Other option," which gives your users the chance to supply responses that are not on the list that you have provided. While this gives them a place to write in their response, it does not function completely like an open-ended question because users generally follow the lead offered by the fixed responses.

OTHER OPTION

Do you own an e-reader?
- ☐ Kindle
- ☐ Nook
- ☐ PocketBook—Sony Reader
- ☐ I don't own an e-book reader
- ☐ Other, please specify [   ]

There are many types of closed-ended question, including the familiar Likert scale.

LIKERT SCALE

How often do you have difficulty finding a space in the library parking lot?
- ☐ Very frequently
- ☐ Somewhat frequently
- ☐ Somewhat infrequently
- ☐ Infrequently
- ☐ Never

Which type you select depends on the purpose of your survey question. Are you asking what users do, think, want, or feel?

What Do Users Do?

Multiple-choice questions with yes/no answers or "Select all that apply" responses are direct ways to ask your users what they do in your library.

Do you participate in library book groups?
- ○ Yes
- ○ No

When you are looking for self-reported data on what your users do, you are typically looking for information that you can't gather in other ways, but in the example given here, the question identifies a subgroup in your survey so that more specific questions can be asked. You may already know how many library users participate in book groups, but by having them self-identify here, you can follow up with the "Yes" respondents to ask book group–specific questions.

Likert scales, which display a range of options, such as "Strongly agree" to "Strongly disagree," are a good tool for users to express how frequently or for how long they do things:

How frequently do you use the library's Web site?

Daily	4–6 times a week	2–3 times a week	Once a week	Less than once a week	Never
O	O	O	O	O	O

When you visit the library, how much time do you estimate you spend doing the following?

	4+ hours	1–3 hours	Less than an hour	I don't do this in the library
Doing schoolwork alone	O	O	O	O
Doing schoolwork in a group	O	O	O	O

What Do Users Think?

Questions that ask users to rank items, such as services or resources, can help identify what they value or see as important. Ranking also can be used to identify user preferences. The value of ranking questions is that they compel the user to make distinctions among the options rather than marking them as all equally pleasing or displeasing.

How would you prefer to learn about future library programs and events? Rank these elements from 1–4.

E-mail	1
Social media	2
Web site	3
Local magazine	4

Likert scales also can elicit what your users think: for example, whether policies are reasonable or unreasonable, or whether hours are adequate or inadequate. Any perception or thought that can be expressed across a gradient—good or bad, useless or useful—can be measured using a Likert scale:

Thinking about the last time you searched for a book at the library, was using the library catalog:

Very easy	Easy	Difficult	Very difficult
○	○	○	○

Sometimes you want your users' thoughts, unconstrained by the options that you offer in your closed-ended questions. Open-ended text entry, though more difficult to interpret, is good when you want to capture reactions and ideas:

Would you like to share additional thoughts on the library's online resources?

What Do Users Want?

Sometimes you have a clear set of options that you, as a library, are exploring. If you ask your users if they'd like them, yes or no, chances are that the majority of users will select "Yes" for each option—if not for themselves, then for others. But such a question format does not adequately reflect the budgets of most libraries, museums, and educational or cultural organizations: We can't provide *all* the options, which is why we are asking the question of our users—which options do you want the most? A ranking option format works well, although you also can simulate constraints by offering a set of options and asking users to pick a specific number:

Which of these renovations to the library building would you prioritize? Rank these elements from 1–4.

Improved lighting	1
Additional small-group study spaces	2
Additional outlets	3
Additional study carrels	4

Which subject areas would you like to see future programming cover?

Local history	1
Popular culture (movies, music . . .)	2
Politics/economics	3
Crafts	4
Literature	5
Technology	6

MULTIPLE CHOICES NEED TO REFLECT
A FULL RANGE OF CHOICES

Closed-ended questions can be frustrating to users when the option that they would like to choose is not there. When reviewing your questions in the testing phase, you can ask your survey testers to consider the range of choices that you are offering. Avoid incomplete or overlapping option ranges like this:

18–24

24–35

40–65

65+

If asking respondents to select from a list of common or well-known items, be sure to include all of the options. For example, this list of fiction genres is incomplete:

Romance

Thriller

Fantasy

What Do Users Feel?

Investigations into our users' feelings are often not part of library surveys, in part because it's not typically what we are inquiring about, but also because there are no readily available conventions for asking questions about feelings. When looking at emotions and feelings, many in marketing and the social sciences would rely on other tools, such as verbal reporting and observation (Tonetto and Desmet, 2012; Scherer, 2005). But it is possible to use verbal scales that reflect feelings to gauge what users feel (Poels and Dewitte, 2006). Users are asked to pick either a dominant feeling or all the feelings that apply in a specific context. To be effective, verbal scales should be designed with an equal range of positive and negative emotions.

We first used verbal scales to measure how our library, as a place, made students feel, but verbal scales also have relevance in areas such as inclusivity, safety, and services.

Thinking of the last time you were in the library, how did you feel? Select all that apply.

☐ Alert
☐ Calm
☐ Confused
☐ Distracted
☐ Efficient
☐ Empowered
☐ Focused
☐ Lost
☐ Overwhelmed
☐ Relaxed
☐ Sleepy
☐ Slow
☐ Smart

AVOIDING THE NEUTRAL OPTION

Likert scales and multiple-choice opinion questions are often written with neutral or "No opinion" options. While the rationale for this appears sound, giving users an out when they don't have an opinion, in reality, such options diminish the amount of useful data collected in surveys. Users satisfice with the neutral option instead of thinking through their preferences. Satisficing is particularly likely toward the end of long questionnaires.

As appealing as offering a no-opinion response may be, doing so may lead researchers to collect less valid and informative data than could be done by omitting it.

—Krosnick et al. (2001)

Draft Language That Is Plain and Clear

When you are composing the actual text of your questions, use plain language. As your users go through your survey, you want them to be reflecting on their own responses, not spending their time deciphering what your questions mean. Ask direct questions with straightforward syntax:

- Have you done *X*?
- Which *Y* do you prefer?

Sometimes questions get complex because you are trying to fit too much into one question. What often results is the double-barreled question:

- Should the library staff receive professional development in virtual reality *and* provide virtual reality tools in the collection?

In cases like this, you want to disentangle the two questions and ask them separately:

- Should the library staff receive professional development in virtual reality?
- Should the library provide virtual reality tools?

Avoiding jargon is also important, especially hidden library jargon that we may overlook because we are so familiar with it. For example, terms like "reference," "circulation," and "collection" by themselves may not mean much to our users. If you need to use specific terms to denote service points or places in the library, many online survey systems allow you to embed photos to provide visual cues in your questions, or provide rollover tool tips for additional explanation.

While you want to guard against unnecessary complexity and jargon as you write your questions, sometimes it slips through despite your best efforts. This is why testing your survey on both internal staff members—especially staff from other departments or units—and external users is so important. They can identify the places in your survey where the language trips them up.

Determine Order

- Start easy.
- Group by topic.

- Limit open-ended questions.
- Request demographic details at either the beginning or the end of the survey.

It's important to give your users the satisfaction of being able to answer the first question or set of questions in your survey competently. As Valerie M. Sue and Lois A. Ritter note in their book *Conducting Online Surveys*, users become more committed to completing a survey the more questions they have answered. Therefore, they argue that the first questions should be "short, simple, and if possible, fun for respondents." "Fun" does not mean frivolous or pointless, but if you are able to identify a question or set of questions that appeals to the respondent's sense of humor or identity, positioning the question early in the instrument may help to engage the respondent.

We've discussed limiting open-ended questions because of the additional coding that they require, but when you do include them, place them at either the end of the relevant section or the end of the survey as a whole. Generally, users consider open-ended questions more challenging, and this allows them to complete the closed-ended questions first. Additionally, answering the closed-ended questions may help call to mind thoughts and perceptions that will aid in responding to the open-ended prompts.

Grouping questions by topic, and even using display cues like page breaks to reinforce this, are important ways that we can prevent confusion in our users. But even the order of individual questions or the order of topics can lead to bias or misunderstanding. Harris (2014) writes that order bias occurs when the response to a question is influenced by the question that came before it. We ran into order bias when we asked about library space first in our survey. To our student respondents, there was nothing provoking about this; but many of our faculty respondents saw it as an indication that we were prioritizing the physical space over our scholarly mission. As a result, their responses in subsequent sections were colored by this fear. Another example where order bias might come into play would be following a question about fines with one about circulation periods. Negative memories about being fined could affect the way that users respond to the second question. If you can identify the potential hot spots in your survey, consider their placement carefully.

Order misunderstanding occurs when the user takes the same frame of reference from the prior question to the next one, even when the questions are explicitly different. For example, a survey that asks about individual behavior and then switches to asking about an entire household may cause order misunderstanding. Consider the frames of reference that you employ in your survey. As you review your survey, group questions by frame and make sure that you clearly indicate when you shift perspectives (Harris 2014). Contextual clauses proferred at the beginning of questions can help guide the reader: "Thinking about the last time . . ." or, "Now we would like to ask about your household's . . ."

Internal Testing and Revision

We recommend at least two iterations of testing. Internal stakeholders, such as other library staff members who are not part of the survey drafting team, are a good group to tap for your first round of testing. Their level of library awareness can help them identify missing options offered in questions, as well as offer language substitutions. With this group, you will want to share the theme and objectives of the survey so that they understand what is to be included and omitted and don't waste time making suggestions that fall outside its parameters.

External Testing and Revision

After you have made the adjustments recommended in the first round, it is time to let some of your users test the survey instrument. With this group, you are looking for points of confusion in the survey, confusing words, and places where they slow down. Observing your users may not be possible, so asking them to address these issues afterward is usually your best bet.

6

Survey Populations

In Chapter 3, we discussed sample size. Planning your survey to ensure that an adequate percentage of people respond is certainly important. However, the size and characteristics of the needed survey respondent pool also relate to the survey's purpose and how the survey data will be used for decision-making. This book's advice applies to large and small surveys alike, but the size of the population invited to respond depends on who can answer the topics covered by the survey.

Thinking carefully about who can provide meaningful information about an issue can help a library determine if a survey is the appropriate tool and whether the information need warrants a large- or small-scale inquiry. Surveys are a common tool for gauging public opinion, and most consumers are inundated by opportunities to take them, especially online. At the same time, many people do not enjoy taking surveys or their tolerance for responding to a survey is limited. While goodwill for the library may drive some people to begin your library's survey, even if they would not respond to a request from a retailer or a political cause, incomplete survey responses are of little use. The design and organization of questions are critical to creating surveys that respondents can complete, but another essential aspect of survey design is matching the survey instrument to the appropriate population of potential respondents.

DEMOGRAPHICS

In most cases, surveys should include a set of demographic questions. As discussed in Chapter 9, demographic information is helpful for data analysis, and examples of demographic questions are included in Appendix A. As noted in Chapter 5, demographic questions are important enough to analysis that we often include them at the beginning of a survey instead of the end in order to ensure that participants respond.

Demographic questions may address gender identity, race, income, level of education, geographic location, family size, or other personal characteristics. The demographic questions included in a survey depend on the research setting (public, academic, school, special, or other type of library); the survey audience; the research question; and how the survey sample size is identified. For example, librarians in a K–12 setting may wish to survey students in a particular grade or school. In this case, asking a question about level of education or geographic location is likely unnecessary. Similarly, librarians who plan to survey employees of an organization may ask respondents to select from a general list of job titles or classifications. Our own library's survey includes a question about whether respondents are students, faculty, instructors, or other staff.

Any demographic questions that you include in your survey deserve careful thought to ensure that respondents are able to make selections that accurately represent their personal information. For questions of race or ethnicity, modeling the options on the U.S. Census may be the most straightforward choice. However, the survey team's knowledge of the library community will help to determine whether the options should be more nuanced. For example, a public library in Hawaii may find that the commonly used option "Native Hawaiian or Pacific Islander" is overly general, and that it would be more accurate to provide additional options to represent specific cultural identities.

The phrasing of demographic questions is also complex because vocabulary changes. Questions of sexual orientation and gender identity exemplify these changes. Surveys conducted in the late 1990s may or may not have included a question about whether a respondent identified as lesbian, gay, bisexual, or transgender (LGBT), but demographic questions about gender identity were not in common use, and "Male" and "Female" were the conventional options. In 2014, we worked with our university's Gender and Sexuality Resource Center to articulate a set of gender identity options that went beyond "Male" and "Female," and "Transgender man" and "Transgender woman" were added. When we deployed the survey again in 2016, we checked in with our colleagues, and they suggested that "Transgender" was sufficient. In essence, demographic distinctions of all kinds are fluid, and they change as cultural sensibilities evolve. If you and your survey team feel unsure about the appropriate demographic options, the best approach is to do some research, consult with local experts, and test draft questions with a small group of library users.

BROAD OR LARGE POPULATIONS

Surveys of large populations are high risk. As a survey designer, you have only a few chances to contact the pool of potential respondents. Survey instruments that are flawed, difficult to understand, or directed at the wrong audience squander the opportunity to learn from the people who respond. Critically, surveys that are too long, difficult to understand, or irrelevant to the respondent's experience may irritate the people who try to respond. While libraries generally enjoy tremendous goodwill in the communities they survey, deploying a flawed survey to a large community is likely to dampen that friendly sentiment. In addition, a survey of any size is useful only if people do respond to it. Bad surveys are likely to have higher rates of discontinuation, which is worse than a low response rate. Libraries can head off these problems through careful planning and design, as explained in previous chapters.

Surveys of broad populations elicit data that may help librarians to generalize about their patron communities and to identify significant trends and their implications for library policies. When surveying a large population, libraries should focus on themes and topics that are applicable to most, if not all, people who could use the library. Convenience, safety, accessibility, and customer service are relevant to any library community, and data about these issues is an asset to program evaluation and planning, especially if the survey is conducted at regular intervals.

While lengthy surveys are rarely advisable, surveys of large populations are often designed to cover multiple themes and topics. When the audience is large, investigators have the latitude to ask a wide range of questions. For example, a diverse survey could cover satisfaction with library customer service, opinions on fairness of borrowing policies, and preferences for library hours and parking. Some people will choose to skip questions, or they will only be able to respond with "Not applicable," but a substantial sample will provide adequate data for most questions.

In our library's biannual survey we use display logic, a common feature of most survey platforms. "Display logic" enables survey designers to tailor the survey experience to specific demographics. In our case, we begin the survey by asking respondents if they are students or employees of the university. Many of the survey questions are the same for both populations, but some differ because students and employees have divergent library experiences. For example, students receive questions about their satisfaction with the library's equipment and study room reservation options because those services are available only to enrolled students in our library, while employees receive questions about their satisfaction with the information literacy instruction sessions that faculty can schedule for their courses. The survey is still distributed to large samples of students and employees, but display logic enables us to deploy only one survey and streamline the survey experience for respondents, asking only questions that are relevant to their experience.

Surveys with a large intended audience can be distributed easily with Web-based survey platforms like Qualtrics, Survey Monkey, or Google Forms; via mail, phone, or fax; at survey kiosks or stations in the library building; or in other ways that are likely to reach a broad cross section of library users. The following are examples of survey questions that could be deployed to a large population served by a library.

Thinking about the last time you visited the library, how did you feel about your safety when entering and exiting the building?

- Concerned
- Somewhat concerned
- Not concerned

→*Why does this question work? Almost all library users could answer it based on their own experience.*

How do you rate the following library services?

	Extremely satisfied	Satisfied	Dissatisfied	Extremely dissatisfied	No basis for judgment
Student equipment checkout	○	○	○	○	○
Group study rooms	○	○	○	○	○
Scanners and copiers	○	○	○	○	○

→*Why does this question work? The question identifies a set of heavily used services offered by a library and also offers respondents the ability to opt out if they have not used a service.*

How do you rate the following library services?

	Extremely satisfied	Somewhat satisfied	Somewhat dissatisfied	Extremely dissatisfied	No basis for judgment
In-person conversation with a library employee	○	○	○	○	○
E-mail with a library employee or department	○	○	○	○	○
Chat/instant message	○	○	○	○	○
Phone	○	○	○	○	○
Social media	○	○	○	○	○

→*Why does this question work? The question identifies a set of heavily used services offered by a library and also offers respondents the ability to opt out if they have not used a service.*

How would you prefer to receive announcements and information about library services, events, and tools? Rank these methods, with 1 being most preferable and 6 being least preferable.

- Library Web site
- Social media (for example, Facebook, Instagram, or Twitter)
- Signs
- Library newsletter
- Talking to a library employee

→*Why does this question work for a large audience? The question offers respondents the chance to rank modes of communication that the library is able to offer. Unlike Likert scales, ranking questions work well for general audiences because they allow people to identify their most preferred option.*

SURVEYS OF SMALL, TARGETED POPULATIONS

Libraries that regularly survey their communities may have a "cast a wide net" philosophy about surveys. This is understandable—why not just put it out there and hope for a strong response rate? Small surveys can be extremely valuable, though. A survey of a small population of library users typically falls into the category of "exploratory research." A survey of a discrete population may help the library to gather practical information about a specific demographic within the community or a particular user group. The insights gained from small surveys may fill a gap in knowledge about an emerging user community or help the library to develop or improve a service, collection, or program. Results from surveys of small, targeted populations of library users can be invaluable tools for decision-making. Library patron communities are dynamic, and information professionals should continually update their knowledge about their growing or emerging constituencies of library users.

Small surveys are a case in which a census is more appropriate than a sample. If you are able to identify all the library users in a target population—for example, all patrons who have reserved a group study room, all professors who teach first-year experience courses, or all patrons enrolled in a monthly book club—a census is a reasonable choice because it is difficult to sample a small population accurately.

Surveys of smaller populations are lower risk because there are fewer potential respondents to annoy or fatigue. While small-scale surveys should be planned and tested just as rigorously as large-scale surveys, they are likely to generate less work at all stages because they may include fewer questions, may cover a more limited scope of topics, and will be distributed to a smaller number of people.

Distribution of small surveys deserves some thought. In the "wide net" model, a library can identify a method of reaching a large sample of users (for example, via e-mail) and deploy the survey using that method. Identifying subsets of the library user population may require some investigation of the kind of data that your library has about your user community. If demographic information is stored in your Integrated Library System (ILS) and you know that you specifically want to survey library users between the ages of 55 and 68, you may be able to extract a report with contact information for that patron group. If the library collects information like "Language spoken at home," a survey for a specific language group could be developed.

Patrons who are signed up to participate in specific library programs are another example of a population that may be easy to identify. For example, patrons involved in a library genealogy course might be the ideal recipients of a survey about planned local history exhibits.

Libraries also can turn to their community partners for assistance in learning about particular populations. For example, a library could collaborate with a social service agency to distribute a survey to its clients about services or programs that they would value. Similarly, a library could partner with area school districts to distribute a survey to families that have registered to home school. Academic libraries may be able to work with their institution's advising, student support, or human resources (HR) offices to identify a demographic of students or employees of the university and distribute a survey to a subset of that population, like international students or students with a disability.

Once identified, survey designers must consider how they will reach a small population. Subsets of a library's community may have limited or no access to the Internet, or they may have personal challenges, like residential instability or immigration concerns, that make them wary of providing a mailing address. Community partners may be able to offer ideas about communication that go beyond e-mailing a survey link. Libraries also should consider surveys that can be responded to via text or Short Message Service (SMS), and surveys delivered on paper, to be filled out on a clipboard or returned with a stamped, self-addressed envelope.

Libraries serving communities where languages other than English are widely spoken should consider translating any survey into the languages spoken by people in the community. If a survey is designed specifically to learn more about library users who speak a language other than English, the questionnaire and all associated material certainly should be translated into that language.

Surveys of library users who have disabilities should be tested to ensure that the instrument is accessible to individuals with disabilities. Web-based survey platforms like Qualtrics offer accessibility checks to determine whether a survey can be read by screen reader tools.

Have you been diagnosed with a disability?

- Yes
- No

[Display logic: If respondent indicates "yes"] Thinking about using the library to get your work done, what are the obstacles that you experience? Please describe.

→*Why does this question work? It gives the respondent the opportunity to self-identify, and then allows those who say "Yes" the opportunity to elaborate.*

Choose the option that best describes your opinion of the following library services.

	Extremely satisfied	Satisfied	Dissatisfied	Extremely dissatisfied	No basis for judgment
I have invited a librarian to visit a class.	○	○	○	○	○
I have suggested or required that a student schedule a consultation with a librarian.	○	○	○	○	○
I have consulted with a library faculty member about my own research.	○	○	○	○	○

→*Why does this question work? It addresses the respondent's specific experience.*

Thinking about your participation in children's programming, how many times a month do you estimate you attend story hour?

	3–4 times per month	1–2 times per month	Rarely	I have never been to story hour
With children I live with at home	○	○	○	○
With children I care for	○	○	○	○

→*Why does this question work? If directed at parents or childcare givers, it presents a realistic scale of frequency and also acknowledges various kinds of adult-child groups that may use library services.*

All surveys designed for specific populations should adhere to the same rigorous standards of planning and testing. A small survey has the same chance of being abandoned if users are confused or burdened by the questions. These surveys may be difficult to execute if the populations are hard to identify; however, they may be shorter and the data will be easier to interpret (though not necessarily generalizable). Libraries are ideal organizations to experiment with small surveys because our user communities are diverse and always changing.

7

Survey Distribution

When you think "survey," you may envision a survey that you have taken online, likely through a platform like Forsee, Google Forms, Qualtrics, Survey Gizmo, Survey Monkey, or even a social media site. Surveys are more accessible to libraries for decision-making than ever before because online survey tools have dramatically reduced the cost of distribution, data collection, and analysis. Most library surveys are, and probably should be, conducted in Web-based settings, though there is a place for questionnaires presented by mail, on the phone, or in person. Creating a survey may be easier and quicker than ever, but the ease of sending a survey online belies the complexity of the options for survey distribution. There is no silver bullet for survey distribution, in libraries or in any field, but two important factors may affect sample size, response rate, and your ability to generalize the results:

- How the invitation to participate is delivered
- Survey format

Online or Web-based surveys are likely the most common form currently used by librarians; however, as you define the population of potential survey participants, consider the ways that they are reachable. Individuals with limited access to the Internet are likely to be excluded from Web-based surveys distributed via e-mail, through a Web site, or on social media. Similarly, public opinion research for decades was conducted primarily by calling residential landlines, but polling organizations have diversified their methods of contacting survey respondents as cell phone ownership has outpaced landline use (McGeeney and Yan 2016). In short, the target audience's behavior and preferences should influence the choice of methods of inviting participation and administering surveys.

SURVEY INVITATIONS: DIRECT VERSUS INDIRECT

Inviting someone to take a survey may sound as simple as posting a link to a Web site or a blog. There are many ways to invite people to participate in a survey, though, and they all succeed to varying degrees. Conventional methods of inviting people can be divided into two basic groups:

Direct Invitations	Indirect Invitations
• Sending e-mail invitations • Mailing out letters • Making phone calls	Posting links to Web sites, blogs, social media pages, listservs, or other online forums

With a direct invitation, potential respondents are specifically identified and asked to participate in the survey. On the other hand, an indirect invitation means that the survey is available to anyone who finds it.

Regardless of the type of invitation you use, you will want to write a message detailing your purpose, what you intend to do with the results, and, ideally, how you intend to share the results with interested respondents. This lets your users know that the survey is not an empty exercise and that you value their input about your operations. Most library surveys pose little or no risk to respondents. Nonetheless, individuals who respond to your survey will appreciate a comment about how their information will be protected. For libraries where survey research is subject to review by an Institutional Review Board, a note about how individual data will be protected is required.

What Should a Survey Invitation Message Say?

The guidelines for what an invitation should say depend on the mode of invitation (as described next). Standard rules of thumb include:

- Use a concise subject line.
- Write a clear message so that the invitation recipient understands the request.
- Provide an accurate estimate of how much time the respondent can expect to take to complete the survey.

- Clearly describe the survey incentives, if applicable.
- Provide contact information if invitation recipients have questions about the survey tool.

Sample invitation text:

Greetings!

[Library name] wants to hear from you! You are invited to take a survey about your satisfaction with library services and programs. If you choose to respond to this survey, your responses will help the library improve and grow. This survey should take less than 7 minutes to complete and will be available until [month, day, year].

Please consider taking the survey linked below:

[https://survey.url]

If you choose to participate in this survey, your responses will be anonymous and no data will be personally identified with you. Participation is completely voluntary, all questions are optional, and you may stop taking the survey any time.

If you choose to participate in this survey, you may choose to enter your e-mail address in a drawing for [survey incentive]. Drawing winners will be contacted by [month, day, year].

If you have questions about [library name]'s survey, you may contact:

Name, title
Phone
E-mail

A survey invitation delivered via text or browser pop-up window should be substantially shorter than an e-mail invitation. For example:

[Library name] values your opinion! Please consider responding to this 3-minute survey:

[https://survey.url]

Whether via e-mail, text, Web browser, letter, phone call, or in-person verbal contact, the context in which you deliver the survey invitation will affect the length and detail of the invitation. However, when you use clear and direct language, respondents will be able to make an informed decision about whether to participate.

When Should I Send My Survey?

It is often said that "timing is everything." Market researchers devote a tremendous amount of energy toward pinpointing the moments at which consumers are most likely to respond to e-mail marketing. When surveys are distributed via e-mail, we recommend choosing times of day during the conventional workweek. The Association of Research Libraries has suggested that Monday and Tuesday are the best days to distribute the LibQUAL+ survey. More flexibly, we suggest that you choose Monday–Thursday, with consideration for what you know about the rhythms and routines of your target audience. Use your Web-based survey platform's e-mail distribution features to schedule an e-mail during the daytime.

How Many Times Should I Send My Survey?

Depending on the length of the survey, as well as how many days or weeks you have until the survey closes, we recommend sending an initial invitation and two to three reminders. The length of time that the survey should be available depends on practical matters like available staff time, not to mention the timeliness of the survey topic. In our experience, one month is a sufficient window of time in which to obtain responses to surveys about library user satisfaction. This may amount to sending one reminder per week until the survey closes. In our experience, the number of survey responses spikes after each reminder. If you use survey platforms like Qualtrics, use the e-mail features to send reminders only to people who have not yet responded, which helps you to avoid sending repeated invitations to people who have already completed the questionnaire. As discussed in Chapter 3, bombarding potential recipients with invitations and pleas to take the survey is unethical, not to mention annoying.

Direct Invitations

E-mail and Text

A common method of directly inviting participants is through e-mail and, increasingly, text messaging. Libraries may have access to user e-mail addresses or cell phone numbers in patron contact information stored in an Integrated Library System (ILS), or from human resources (HR), a registrar's office, or another administrative unit. Libraries within organizations that provide e-mail addresses to students, employees, or other affiliates may have an easier time accessing their users' e-mail addresses than do public libraries. However, having an e-mail address does not mean that people read or respond to e-mail. In polls conducted by the Pew Research Center, the number of Americans who say that they "go online" daily is 89 percent, a rate that has continued to increase every year for over a decade (Perrin and Jiang 2018). Libraries are hubs for going online, particularly for people who do not have residential Internet access, but that does not guarantee that patrons will prioritize responding to surveys while using library devices or Wi-Fi. In addition, various reports indicate that some demographics prefer text messages and social media to e-mail (Duggan 2013), and experiments by the Pew Research Center indicate that people invited to take a survey by text respond more quickly than those invited by e-mail (McGeeney and Yan 2016). While not all libraries will have access to patron e-mail and cell phone numbers, those that do should consider both the way a survey invitation is delivered and the ways in which people can respond (online, in print, verbally, etc.).

Surveys distributed via e-mail or text offer libraries control over the sample size. For example, a library that maintains user e-mail addresses in patron accounts could deploy the survey to a subset of the patron population with valid e-mail addresses. A library might e-mail or text a customer satisfaction survey to any user who has just completed a transaction in the library or to a certain percentage of users who completed a transaction during a defined period of time.

Deploying surveys via e-mail or text excludes nonusers of the library or users who have not disclosed their e-mail or mobile phone numbers to the library. E-mail surveys also may exclude populations with limited or no access to the Internet, people who do not have e-mail addresses, and/or people who are not in the habit of checking their e-mail. In this context, libraries affiliated with educational institutions are at an advantage because they have access to student and/or parent e-mail addresses through the institution's registrar, campus technology services, or the ILS. Public libraries may be able to access e-mail addresses maintained by municipal governments, and e-mail addresses based on ZIP codes or other geographic characteristics can be purchased from market research firms. However, all libraries should consider whether e-mail and text are sufficient and appropriate mechanisms for survey distribution.

Pop-up Windows

Have you ever visited a Web site at which you received a pop-up survey invitation? Surveys delivered in this way can fall into the "direct invitation" category if the Web site has been coded so that a pop-up window appears for a random subset or for all Web visitors. These windows are usually set to appear based on Internet Protocol (IP) address, but they also could be set to appear when a user logs into his or her library account or authenticates in some way. Many Internet users disable pop-up windows, and even when they do not, these surveys are easily dismissed.

However, a pop-up window could appear when a user accesses a specific library resource or an online service like chat or instant messaging. These surveys have the advantage of collecting feedback from an active library user and are often pinpointed to ask about the user's most recent experience. A survey like this also can collect data indefinitely or over a long period of time, to be analyzed at regular intervals for decision-making.

Letters and Phone Calls

Surveys were long conducted without the Web, and they still are. Surveys sent through the mail or administered over the phone are costly in terms of money and time. However, a library that maintains patron contact information may choose to administer the survey to a sample of patrons who are more likely to respond via mail or phone. Letters also can be used as a method of distributing the online Uniform Resource Locator (URL) of a survey, but keep in mind that this method, which asks the user to type the URL into a device to which they have access, may have a low rate of follow-through. Typically, libraries use this method in conjunction with e-mail and Web campaigns.

In-Person Approach

Surveys can be conducted in person as well. Whether at a polling place, in an airport, or at a library, prospective respondents can be approached and invited to take a survey. Earlier in this chapter, we mentioned that libraries could e-mail or text a customer satisfaction survey to every patron who checks out an item—or to every fifth or seventh patron, for that matter. Similarly, patrons could respond to a satisfaction survey on paper or a mobile device after they complete a transaction, or library staff could ask if they would consent to receive a survey via e-mail or text. Library users can be invited to respond to surveys at reference desks, or survey stations could be set up at library entrance and exit points. Surveys also may be distributed to people using a particular space in the library, like study tables or public access computers. If library staff members are able to approach library users and hand them a piece of paper or a tablet with a survey on the screen, they have the advantage of capturing the opinion of people who are actively using the library at a given moment. On the other hand, this approach likely excludes patrons who primarily use Web-based services, as well as inactive library users.

Indirect Invitations

Posting Links

Libraries can distribute surveys by posting links to Web sites, social media accounts, or e-mail listservs, relying on interested parties to opt in when they see a link. The advantage to this kind of survey is that it can be distributed to anyone who interacts with the library online. Such a survey may attract a panel of active users who are visiting the library Web site, using the catalog, or following the library's social media feeds. However, distributing a survey by posting a link to a Web site almost certainly excludes active library users who rarely or never interact with the library online, whether by choice or circumstance. While all surveys conducted by libraries depend on self-selecting respondents, the library users who notice the survey link and choose to respond in that moment do not compose a representative sample, making it harder for you to generalize the results across your user population.

Other problems with surveys distributed in this way are that respondents may include library employees or individuals with a particular agenda related to the survey's intent, Internet users who are not members of the library's community, or survey-taker bots set up to crawl the Internet and automatically fill in forms. "Ballot box stuffing" is also a concern with surveys that are linked to Web sites and freely available to any Web visitor. Some survey platforms have tools to prevent a respondent from taking a survey repeatedly, and libraries also may consider requiring respondents to authenticate as a patron before the survey opens. The disadvantage of the latter approach may be that respondents may move on because they do not feel like logging in.

The greatest problem with indirect surveys is that the results are not derived from a random sample because they come from respondents who happened to see the survey opportunity. While the people who choose to respond may seem random, the term "random sample" means that "selections are drawn from a population in a way that gives every member and every combination of members an equal chance of being selected" (Johnson 2000, 283). If the respondents encountered the survey invitation by circumstance, not because the researchers intended to invite them, they do not comprise a random sample of the population. For example, librarians who subscribe to e-mail listservs have ample opportunities to respond to survey invitations distributed through professional e-mail lists. The problem with distributing a survey through a listserv or social media group is that the membership is not necessarily representative of the demographics of the target audience.

Surveys like this create a "nonprobability sample" of participants, which may not be representative of the whole user community. A recent study explored statistical methods that may help to reduce bias within data collected through opt-in instruments (Mercer, Lau, and Kennedy, 2018). These methods employ a level of statistical rigor that is likely outside the skill set of most library professionals, and current research indicates that controlling for bias remains extremely difficult with opt-in panels. Any organization may still conclude that posting a survey to its Web site and social media pages is the best way to invite participants. If that is the best or only way, researchers should be aware and acknowledge that the results may not be representative or generalizable. However, that does not mean that the survey results lack all value.

SURVEY PLATFORMS

Web-Based Surveys

The proliferation of low-cost tools for building questionnaires has enabled libraries to seek patron opinions with greater frequency than ever. Unlike surveys issued on paper, online surveys collect respondent data that can usually be downloaded as a spreadsheet and analyzed with a variety of tools. Web-based surveys can be constructed to display the same questions to all recipients; however, many online survey platforms allow the survey designer to present different versions of a survey depending on how the survey taker responds using the same instrument. For example, a satisfaction survey could offer different questions to different demographics of survey respondents. A library at a college or university might develop a survey with some questions designed for staff and faculty and other questions for students; or a federated library system could allow respondents to select their primary public library and integrate questions specific to that library's distinct offerings.

Accessibility is a crucial consideration with Web-based survey tools. Just as libraries strive to publish Web sites that are accessible to people who are blind or visually impaired, Web-based library surveys should meet or exceed current accessibility standards. Some survey platforms offer accessibility check tools to determine if a survey is compatible with screen reader software. Concerns about accessibility also can be addressed by diversifying the formats of survey distribution in order to be as inclusive of a library's community as possible.

Paper

Paper surveys present substantial administrative obstacles. Transferring a survey response from paper to a spreadsheet or database opens opportunities for data entry errors, and it takes time to boot. A key factor in deciding whether to conduct a paper survey should be whether the library can spare the staff, intern, or volunteer time needed to tabulate the survey results. Some libraries may have the option of using machine-readable paper survey instruments from companies like Scantron, but the cost may be prohibitive. Tablet computers are sometimes used as quasi-paper surveys: the survey administrator provides a person with a tablet, and the participant responds and returns the tablet. The tablet application collects the responses in a spreadsheet. Just as accessibility is a concern with Web-based surveys, surveys administered on paper or on a tablet may not be accessible.

Paper surveys also can be distributed by mail if the patron addresses and funds for postage and printing are available. In addition to the costs and challenges of data entry, surveys distributed by mail are considerably more expensive than online surveys because of the cost of postage. Public libraries may be able to work with local government to access residential addresses in order to send surveys to a large population. Libraries also might think opportunistically about partnering with municipal agencies, like recreational departments or utilities, to include a survey with material that those agencies plan to mail. Then comes the matter of collecting and tabulating the data for analysis.

No survey distribution tool is perfect. As you plan your survey, you are most likely to use Web-based tools to build it and to invite prospective respondents. We simply advise that you think carefully about how your methods align with the purpose of your survey.

8

Analysis of Results

Readers of this book probably work in libraries, not market research firms or public opinion polling organizations. Typically, after a survey closes, a new phase begins: data analysis, followed by decision-making (Chapter 9). Designing and deploying a survey are exciting, and perusing the survey results, especially as they flow in, sparks inspiration and discussion. As you plan your survey, building in time for survey analysis is essential or else you risk forming conclusions based on superficial impressions from cherry-picked results. Speaking from our own experience, cherry-picking is easy to do. In this chapter, we lay out some steps that will help you analyze your data intentionally so that you can make good decisions based on the evidence that you have worked hard to gather.

PRELIMINARY WORK

Remember your survey plan (Chapter 2)? Analysis should be driven by the theme and objectives of the survey. To be sure, surveys may reveal unexpected conclusions that open up new avenues for inquiry. However, your initial analysis should focus on the questions that you sought to answer when you planned the survey. As information professionals, we know that statistics and data are easily misinterpreted. A clear theme and logical objectives will help you extract descriptive statistics that will inform meaningful conclusions.

QUANTITATIVE DATA

After your survey has closed, you can begin your analysis by producing descriptive statistics for each question. Descriptive statistics can inform several types of survey data analysis:

- Frequency, or how many: 62 percent check out books for more than one member of their household.
- Charts, graphs, or other visualizations: These demonstrate trends or compare data for different years or user groups.
- Characterization of the "typical": 80 percent of students believe that the collection meets their needs.
- Comparison between two or more groups: 80 percent of students believe that the collection meets their needs, while 45 percent of instructors believe that the collection meets their needs.
- Correlations, or relationships, between data: Preferences for collection formats, by age and income level.

When you begin, we recommend that you analyze questions in at least two phases. During the first pass, attempt to identify key descriptive statistics quickly. In the second pass, think more deeply about the results and attempt to relate questions to each other. If you have created a long survey, this may sound overwhelming. Dividing your survey into sections

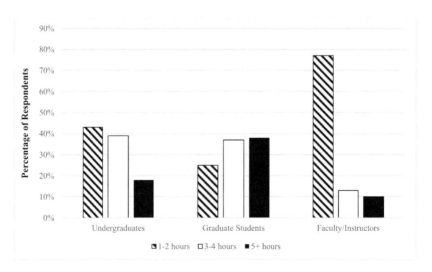

FIGURE 8.1. Estimated Average Length of a Visit to the Library

or scopes, as we suggest in Chapter 4, not only helps with organization, but also in identifying tasks for analysis. This process is also easier if you have used a survey distribution platform like Qualtrics or Survey Monkey because these tools, though fee based, perform some of the basic analysis, including generation of visualizations.

You are not likely to be a neutral analyst of your library's survey results. Nonetheless, if you find yourself feeling defensive about the results, remember that you asked the question, so prepare to accept the responses. One way to approach negative survey responses is to adjust your expectations. On questions of satisfaction, remember that some level of discontent is inevitable. Your analysis should help you determine whether rates of dissatisfaction require a response or a change. On questions of preference, be alert for surprises and challenges to your assumptions.

Strategies for Analysis

Purpose: Gauge patron satisfaction with library policies.

Question: The library's fines and fees are fair and appropriate.

Strongly agree: 2 percent

Agree: 20 percent

Neutral: 55 percent

Disagree: 15 percent

Strongly disagree: 8 percent

First pass:

- 22 percent of people do not object to our fines and fees.
- 23 percent of people do object to our fines and fees.
- 55 percent of respondents are neutral about our fines and fees.

Second pass:

- Clustering the "Neutral," "Agree," and "Strongly agree" responses shows that in general, patron sentiments about this issue are *not* negative.
- More than half of the respondents are neutral about fines and fees. Does this mean they don't have any experience with our late policy?

Looking at the next question offers additional insights:

Question: Library books can be checked out for 21 days, and DVDs can be checked out for 7 days. Please select the statement that most reflects your experience:

- I never borrow anything because I don't have enough time: 7 percent
- I have difficulty returning materials before the due date: 8 percent
- I always try to renew materials because I need more time: 32 percent
- I usually manage to finish before the due date: 40 percent
- The borrowing periods are sufficient: 13 percent

First pass:

- Most people have no trouble using materials within the current borrowing schedule.

Second pass:

- A substantial number say that they want more time to borrow materials.
- The number of people who are neutral about fines and fees is close to the number who do not object to the existing borrowing periods. This may mean they are not familiar with the library's fines and fees.

Conclusion: People who are unfamiliar with fines and fees do not object to our present borrowing periods, but people who have incurred fees do object. Additional data may be needed in order to make a decision.

Purpose: Identify the preferred instructional approaches for online learners.

Question: In what areas do you believe online writing students would benefit most from library intervention? (Please rank.)

	Ranking	Total
Understanding source types	1	37
Developing a research question	2	31
Selecting a topic	3	29
Developing a search strategy	4	26

	Ranking	Total
Identifying different "voices" in the conversation	5	14
Evaluating sources for authority and value	6	8
Conducting background research	7	2

First pass:

The top-ranked options are

- Understanding source types
- Developing a research question

The bottom-ranked options are

- Evaluating sources for authority and value
- Conducting background research

Second pass:

- "Understanding source types" is ranked well above all the other options.
- Options 2, 3, and 4 are ranked close together, followed by a significant drop-off.
- Options 1–4 appear to be the highest priorities of instructors.

Analysis with Cross-Tabulation

The survey samples in this book include specific questions about demographics. Demographic questions are certainly helpful in developing profiles of users. More important, demographic questions are a key tool in survey analysis. Web-based tools like Survey Monkey and Qualtrics allow cross-tabulation of most results without requiring you to do much, if any, math.

Purpose: Learn more about how students conduct research.

Question: If you were assigned a research paper for which you had to obtain scholarly or peer-reviewed literature, which of the following things would you do first?

	Percentage	Total
Google it	36	48
Search the library home page	45	59
Ask a professor for recommendations	11	15
Ask a librarian for recommendations	0.76	1
Other	7	9

First pass:

- Students do not start their research by asking a librarian.
- Students like Google.

Second pass:

Cross-tabulate, based on year in school.

	Google	Library	Professor	Librarian
First year	21	5	0	0
Second year	13	8	4	0
Third year	5	17	5	1
Fourth year	5	18	6	0
Fifth year and later	5	11	0	0

- The largest number of respondents begin either with the library home page or a search engine.
- A substantial number of students ask their instructors for help.
- More first-year students begin with Google than any other group.
- Library use increases as students advance through schooling.

Conclusion: Students prefer to start a project independently before they ask for help. Students rely on their professors for guidance, so the library should dedicate marketing and outreach efforts toward ensuring that professors refer students to the library. First-year students appear to be less aware of the library than third- and fourth-year students.

Purpose: Understand how the library's physical environment affects library users.

Question: How do you feel about your safety when visiting the library?

	Concerned	Somewhat Concerned	Not Concerned
Arriving during the day	4%	0%	96%
Arriving at night	11%	0%	89%
Departing during the day	2%	0%	98%
Departing at night	22%	32%	46%
Studying in the library during the day	2%	0%	98%
Studying in the library at night	4%	4%	92%

First pass:

- Users are not concerned about their safety when they enter, spend time in, or exit the library during the day.
- Users are concerned about their safety leaving the library at night.

If you ask users to complete some demographic questions, preferably at the beginning of the survey, you will be able to cross-tabulate the results for more sophisticated analysis.

	Studying in the Library at Night			Departing the Library at Night		
	Concerned	Somewhat Concerned	Not Concerned	Concerned	Somewhat Concerned	Not Concerned
Man	2	8	87	3	8	85
Woman	187	155	29	247	105	1
Transgender	2	0	0	2	0	0
Other	0	0	1	0	0	1
Decline to state	0	2	2	0	0	4

Second pass:

- Cross-tabulation shows that library users whose gender identity is not male are more concerned about their safety.
- The majority of respondents who identify as female are somewhat concerned about their safety when leaving the library at night.
- Although less than 1 percent of all survey respondents identified as transgender, 100 percent of transgender respondents indicated nighttime safety concerns. Users who selected "Other" or "Prefer not to state" appear to have different concerns. Further research is needed.

Conclusion: Evening safety is a concern for a substantial number of the library's users.

Analysis of Trends

Surveys conducted once offer a snapshot, or a point-in-time, view of an issue. Surveys administered at intervals offer you the chance to analyze trends or test the effect of a change or intervention.

Question: If you were assigned a research paper for which you had to obtain scholarly or peer-reviewed literature, which of the following things would you do first?

	2016	2017	2018
Google it	36%	37%	36%
Search the library home page	44%	43%	48%
Ask a professor for recommendations	11%	8%	9%
Ask a librarian for recommendations	0.76%	5%	6%
Other	7%	7%	1%

First pass:

- The rate of asking a librarian increased from the first year to the second.
- The rate of searching the library home page increased from the first and second years to the third.
- Search engine use remained stable.

Second pass:

- A campaign to encourage instructors to direct students to the library may have a positive effect.
- The library home page was redesigned last year, and increase in use since then may reflect improved usability.

QUALITATIVE DATA

If your survey includes free-form comments, you may be able to recognize some trends and patterns immediately. To get an objective sense of the ideas and opinions reflected in these comments, it is best to code them. If qualitative responses come from an "Other" option, the coded results should be analyzed in relation to the quantitative question. For questions that include an open-ended or free-form option, coded data also should be analyzed in relation to the same question's quantitative result. In some cases, this may reveal that respondents misunderstood the question or options. The coded, free-form comments also may demonstrate that respondents have additional categories of experience that you had not previously observed. Further, qualitative responses may come from a concluding question such as, "Please share any additional thoughts about the library's collections." In this case, the coded responses may relate to any quantitative question about the collections, but you will not know this until you have coded the data.

By coding open-ended comments, you can distill user sentiments into their most significant messages and then aggregate the number of people who share those messages. It also helps remove the emotional aspect of reading subjective comments, which can cause you to overaccentuate comments that seem more emphatic or significant. For example, a survey about the library building may elicit many negative comments about the public restrooms. Learning that your users think that the library's restrooms are "disgusting," "gross," "dirty," and "repulsive" may seem alarming. These comments can be distilled to "restrooms—dissatisfied" in order to reflect the essence of the sentiment and tabulate the frequency that this opinion is expressed. In effect, through coding, you are quantifying your qualitative responses.

In the social sciences, there are many methods for coding qualitative responses, and they are used for both surveys and interviews. Many of these methods tend to be more complex than is really necessary for a library survey. We must regularize the respondent's meaning to count, analyze, and contextualize qualitative responses. What we propose is an adaptation of a descriptive coding method for free-form qualitative responses, as described by Saldaña (2016). Coding is a relatively time-consuming process; for this reason, we strongly urge you to limit the number of open-ended or free-form questions in your survey.

With descriptive coding, you want to assign a phrase (or word) that captures the meaning of a comment or part of a comment. Because descriptive coding is usually generated spontaneously, you can't rely on a ready-made thesaurus of appropriate terms. Part of the trick of descriptive coding is that you want to harmonize your codes as you go along, or else in a second pass-through. For example, while coding a collection of more than 100 comments, we initially assigned the following codes to comments about wayfinding and signage in the library:

- More signage
- Neg signage
- Better signage

After reviewing the codes, we revised them all to "Improve signage." When making such revisions, you should test, by looking at the original comment, that you are still accurately reflecting its meaning. The level of granularity in your coding depends on both how you intend to use the comments and the specificity of the comments that you receive. In the case of our signage comments, they were not rich in detail, but instead were broad complaints about lack of signs and directions. While we would not be using the comments to diagnose the specifics of our wayfinding problem, we could use them in the aggregate to demonstrate the prevalence of the issue for our users. Codes can be misapplied or consolidated to the point of losing their usefulness. For example, collapsing comments about navigating the library Web site with comments about difficulty accessing Wi-Fi would conflate two different issues into one broad category.

Often, responses to open-ended questions will reflect multiple sentiments. To capture what are often disparate ideas, it is a good idea to give each one its own code:

Original Comment	Code 1	Code 2	Code 3
More vending machines. Control the heat better. Fix the outlets. They suck.	HVAC	More vending machines	Outlets

While it may seem to overrepresent the positions of those who give compound responses, remember that even when coded and quantified, open-ended responses do not represent votes or enfranchisement, but merely expressions of feelings and ideas for you to consider. In the majority of surveys, open-ended questions are answered by a fraction of the total survey-taking user group. Weighing the significance of the responses is difficult. On the one hand, taking the time and effort to comment often indicates a real desire to communicate the thoughts expressed. On the other, it is very hard to gauge whether and how those thoughts represent those of the larger population.

Coded data from open-ended questions is valuable when it reveals more detail about a quantitative trend. In our own library's survey, we found that students were enthusiastic about the library's quiet zones. In one set of coded comments, we found that 7 percent of all the comments received were about patron preferences for the quiet zones, including a desire for greater enforcement of quiet-zone rules. While the quantitative data confirmed that users liked our quiet areas, the number of qualitative comments gave us convincing insights.

Sometimes open-ended comments can serve as the seeds for a future survey question or other research inquiry. For example, when we received numerous comments about the cold temperatures in the library, we realized that this aspect was missing from our questions about the library as a space. Open-ended responses sometimes also reveal misunderstandings that point to necessary revisions of future survey instruments. For example, we have asked patrons what "obstacles to using the library" they experienced, and our intent was to understand the challenges posed by our library space for individuals with disabilities. But the responses included statements like "I feel sleepy in the library" or "I see friends and end up socializing instead of studying." In subsequent versions of the survey, we revised the question to target a subset of all survey respondents, as a screening question: "Have you been diagnosed with a disability?" To respondents who said yes, we asked, "How would you describe your disability or disabilities? Select all that apply:

- A sensory impairment (related to vision or hearing)
- A mobility impairment or limitation
- A learning disability (e.g., ADHD, dyslexia)
- A mental health condition
- A disability or impairment not listed above"

These two questions helped frame the question about obstacles and also helped us analyze the results by cross-tabulating disabilities with accessibility concerns.

We assume that librarians who are designing their own survey instruments are likely also taking on the task of analyzing their survey results. Survey analysis is laborious, but when a survey is well designed, the reward is a set of reliable conclusions that can support evidence-based decision-making. While there is no formula for a mix of quantitative and qualitative questions, surveys that are mostly quantitative lend themselves to more efficient analysis. Libraries value the perspectives of individuals, so learning how to code open-ended responses creates a rich set of data that compliments and supports the information collected from quantitative questions.

9

Taking Action

It can be tempting, after reviewing and analyzing your survey results, to rest on your new knowledge. There are many reasons to delay your survey follow-through. Whether your survey is a brief, focused questionnaire about a single topic or a more expansive one about your entire operation, it can be daunting to turn its results, which may not all be conclusive, into concrete steps or goals. Or perhaps the results suggest changes whose implementations depend on new funding, institutional approval, or buy-in from your board. After the excitement of collecting user responses, it is very common to feel a letdown. Turning your results into action is one of the hardest parts of the survey process.

Acting on your survey results is about more than what you will do in your library—the decisions and changes that you make as a result of your findings. It is also about how you will communicate those results to your staff, administrators, and partners, as well as how you will report them to your library users. This phase in the survey process offers an opportunity for meaningful engagement with both staff and users. Sharing survey results, generating or discussing planned improvements, and receiving further feedback reinforce how you value library stakeholders. In fact, communicating both your results and your plans is crucial not just for sharing information with your staff and users, but also for increasing buy-in to the process, creating more ideas, and serving as a valuable check on your analysis of your survey findings.

A typical workflow after analyzing your results is an iterative process of sharing and planning, communicating, and making decisions. Depending on the complexity of your survey, your library, and the number of stakeholders invested in its subject matter, you might go through multiple

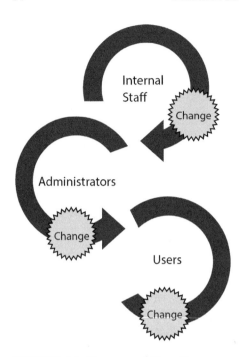

FIGURE 9.1. Process of Iterative Communication and Change

rounds of sharing, but the basic pattern is dialogue followed by change. The formality or informality of this process has a lot to do with your audiences and your purposes in communicating with them. For example, when discussing survey results with internal staff, you may be looking for the unique insights that the circulation department staff might have on why satisfaction levels for their unit are so high. Keeping discussions informal and discursive helps elicit interpretive reflections from staff who might not speak up at a more formal, presentation-style meeting. Conversely, more structure might be needed if you are sharing survey results with your staff or administration as the rationale for making significant changes in your library. Library users are quite a different audience. Typically, communicating survey results to library users tends to be less dialogic and more like reporting, simply because of the ways that we reach our users. Even so, there are ways to signal both your library's openness to further feedback and the value that you place on users' reflections.

MAKING DECISIONS

Making decisions on the basis of survey findings is a responsibility that can fall to different people or groups, depending on your library and the nature of your survey. If you are part of the team who designed your survey, you may not necessarily be part of the decision-making process that emerges based on your survey results. A lot depends on the purpose and context of your surveys. For example, a library director interested in planning a capital project may propose doing a survey in order to understand patron feelings about the library's facility. The group that plans and administers the survey may turn over the results and analysis without having any input on the director's future plans. In the case where the survey team passes results on to other committees, department heads, or directors, it is important that the survey team shares and explains both its data and its analysis. The team members' expertise at that point in the process will help keep decision-makers from blundering into some of the pitfalls that we have discussed in this book, which are common to a first reading of survey data.

Short, single-focus surveys don't present as much difficulty when it comes to making decisions and taking action. If your results point to a clear preference or sentiment among your users, you have your response to your survey objective. But sometimes, even in a tightly focused survey, the results are more ambiguous. When your results reveal heterogeneous interests, especially those related to collections or programming, you have evidence of the complexity of your library community. When there is no agreement among your users and the response to your query seems to be a draw, other factors may inform your response to the research question. These could include internal data mined from your Integrated Library System (ILS), gate counts, computer logons, event attendance, and staffing or budgetary information, as well as external data from government agencies like the U.S. Census, school district, and housing and transit authorities.

Longer, more complex surveys are significantly harder to turn their results from data into action. While the purpose of your survey may be as clear as helping plan a new space in the library or as diffuse as informing your strategic planning process, longer surveys often reveal additional actionable information beyond survey objectives. As a result, managing the ideas and decisions that arise when interrogating the survey data becomes a more involved process of prioritization and delegation. The urgency of knowing your users' wishes and desires is often tempered by the constraints faced when making change.

Decisions emerging from a successful survey can be internal, involving budgeting, staffing, or programming, for example. Or they can be external, involving change with community partners, consortia, or even transportation services. And while you certainly can encounter some holdups even in successful collaborations with external partners, sometimes your internal decisions are held up by factors such as administrator approval, the budget cycle, or staffing.

If a number of decisions emerge from your survey, you also face time constraints. It is usually impossible to tackle everything at once. An implementation schedule can help you plan and track your progress. It also can keep you from losing track of initiatives that might be months or years in your future. Furthermore, if your decisions are a combination of brief "to do" items and more involved projects, mapping them all out can help you keep from focusing on your "to dos" at the expense of your projects. Here is a sample implementation schedule:

June

Investigate scheduling software options for room reservations.

Refresh signage for quiet zones.

Consult with facilities on lighting options.

July

Propose three-year plan for lighting renovation.

Plan programming for the fall.

August

Consider reallocating funds for room reservation software.

Tabled: Plan staff customer service trainng.

Delegated:

Physical Plant

Temperature issues

Sound of chiller

Custodial Services

Bathroom stall locks

Management Team:

Meet with development staff.

COMMUNICATING ABOUT YOUR RESULTS

How you present your survey results depends a lot on your audiences. Are you sharing your results with the rest of the staff, looking for their feedback? Or are you using the results to demonstrate the need for change? If you're presenting to administrators or a board of directors, you may be seeking to demonstrate the strengths of your library, even as you pitch the changes that your survey has inspired. When you're reporting back to your users, very often you are showing how their valuable input has led to real and tangible changes. But regardless of which audience you are addressing, turning survey results into cogent and identifiable messages is a real challenge.

It has become axiomatic that if you want to connect with an audience, you need to learn to tell your story. This advice is given to companies, non-profits, job-seekers, and even individuals interested in personal growth.

It may seem out of place in a section about sharing survey results, but thinking in terms of stories can help you frame survey data into manageable and memorable chunks. As someone who has participated in the designing, implementation, or analysis of your survey, you have probably already constructed narratives about your results. Familiarity with the objectives, the choice of survey population, and other background information that went into the design and analysis of the survey can help you provide context and connections between the points of data. Working to make these narratives explicit for your audience will help you compose a more meaningful message. As Donald Polkinghorne (1988, 1) notes in *Narrative Knowing and the Human Sciences,* narrative is "the primary form by which human experience is made meaningful." Framing your results as stories can help your audience find purchase with the information you are sharing, whether it be in presentation, document, or infographic form.

The process of turning your results into a story is largely about making choices. As Robert McKee (1997, 33) says in *Story: Substance, Structure, Style, and the Principles of Screenwriting,* the structure of a story "is a selection of events," ordered strategically. While McKee is speaking of a different kind of story than one that we might tell about our survey data, the principle remains the same. While survey data by itself does not seem at all like the plot of a story like *The Wizard of Oz,* the analysis of that data presents multiple "events" that are worthy of organizing and presenting. Changes in preferences, behavior, or satisfaction are always compelling events to highlight, but your stories need not all be about contrast or change. Drawing connections among pieces of data also works, as does bringing survey responses into relationships with data collected through other means, like your Integrated Library System (ILS), or qualitative data collected through interviews, focus groups, or observational studies. If you have collected demographic data as part of your survey, the intersection of user categories with responses in your cross-tabulation analysis is another story that you can tell.

Here are some examples of stories that you can tell about survey data:

Data: Responses about the availability of laptops, outlets, quality of Wi-Fi, and ease of mobile printing.

Story: The decrease in desktop computers has put a demand on our infrastructure for supporting laptops and mobile devices.

Action item: Create a plan to address equipment support needs.

Data: An attendance and satisfaction matrix about adult programing options.

Story: The majority of our programming was well liked in our 55+ demographic, but the popularity of sustainable living classes and salary negotiation workshops with patrons 18–35 represents an outreach opportunity.

Action item: Increase programming targeted to younger demographics.

Data: Quantitative and qualitative questions reflecting incomplete knowledge of the library space and frustration with locating resources.

Story: Users can't find or aren't aware of key resources in the library, pointing to the need for a revised wayfinding system.

Action item: Evaluate existing signage and allocate resources to improve signage in the next fiscal year.

An important caution: Although we're telling stories about our data, we are not trying to write fiction. Make sure that the messages you share with your audiences are supported by your data. Any claims that you can't connect back clearly to your survey results are purely editorial and subjective.

It may seem obvious, but the stories that you share with your internal staff, administrators, or users will not necessarily be the same. To your staff and administrators, you may be both sharing your results and asking them to initiate, approve, or fund a change. Rhetorically, it pays to present more than just the negatives that your survey reveals. You want to combine messages about the value that the library already offers with information about the changes that you want to make to improve it.

Sharing survey results with extremal users presents its own unique challenges. For one thing, the methods for reaching out to users are limited. For example, you can't call a meeting with your users. Typically, libraries share their survey results in the form of a written report or summary on their Web site. Another way of conveying selected survey highlights to your users is through the use of infographics, which can be shared easily via social media, in newsletters, and in the library. It also can be effective to refer back to your survey when informing your users about changes or new services or resources that result from their input. This provides the rationale behind your decisions, but it also impresses upon your users the value of providing input. If they know that their responses matter, they are more likely to respond to your next request for feedback.

THE BARE MINIMUM

It is better to figure out a way to communicate some, or even a little, rather not communicate about your survey at all. Consigning your survey results to the dustbin, without ever sharing them with your staff and users, is a good way of depleting the value of using surveys at all. Any decisions made based on a survey, but not connected to it, lose the imprimatur of being data driven. But perhaps more significant, staff members are likely to become suspicious of the practice of deploying surveys, seeing them as tools that go nowhere. Thinking back to Chapter 3 and the reasons that people choose to respond to surveys, the ego-driven desire to make a positive contribution to an organization that one values may be sufficient motivation to devote time to a library survey. If that is the case, respondents may hope to learn how the survey turned out. And users, already prone to survey fatigue in our feedback-hungry culture, may be less likely to participate in future surveys if they feel that their contribution served no purpose.

The following information indicates what we see as the minimum communication practices that should be implemented after completing a survey, along with ideas for sharing your results more thoroughly.

Recommended communication practices after surveys:

Minimum for internal audiences:

- Executive summary

More comprehensive options:

- Presentations
- Workshops
- Share data such as exported sets of results or executive summaries
- Infographics
- Share implementation schedule/proposed changes

Minimum for users:

- Short Web posting

More comprehensive:

- Multiple Web postings, or a more complete Web page detailing the survey results
- Infographics online and in the library
- Messaging with new services/products (for example, mobile book carts, streaming video)

In Chapter 2, we emphasized the importance of planning, calling on the principles of design thinking to help you use empathy to design a survey instrument that respondents understand and to which they can respond authentically. Design thinking is conventionally applied to the development of commercial products, customer experiences, and architectural spaces, and survey data is often collected and analyzed as part of that process. While we stated earlier that you must empathize with your survey respondents, we urge you to use your survey results to develop empathy with your library community as well. As we have argued in this chapter, the data collected in your survey can help your library take action and chart a path forward with small and large library initiatives.

Appendix A

Sample Demographic Questions

GENDER, AGE, RACE, ETHNICITY, AND LANGUAGE

With which gender do you currently identify?

- Woman
- Man
- Transgender
- Other
- Decline to state

What is your age?

- 18–24
- 25–30
- 31–40
- 41–50
- 51–65
- 66+

Are you White, Black or African American, American Indian or Alaskan Native, Asian, Native Hawaiian or other Pacific islander, or some other race?

- White
- Black or African American

- American Indian or Alaska Native
- Asian
- Native Hawaiian or other Pacific Islander
- Two or more races
- Other

Note: Based on what you know about your community and the level of granularity you want in your results, you may want to adjust this list. For example, "Native Hawaiian or other Pacific Islander" may not be specific enough if you are surveying a library community in Hawaii or Guam.

Are you Hispanic or Latino?

- Yes
- No

What is the primary language you currently speak?

Note: The options associated with this question should be based on the primary languages spoken within the library community. This list may be easy to produce based on the languages spoken by your library's staff and patrons; however, in the United States, Census data is readily available to consult for a sense of the languages spoken in the library service area. This question also may be adjusted based on your survey audience. For example, a school library may ask parents, "What is the primary language spoken in your home?"

HOUSEHOLD SIZE

How many children under the age of 18 reside in your home?

- None
- 1
- 2
- 3 or more

How many adults over the age of 18 reside in your home?
- None
- 1
- 2
- 3 or more

INCOME

What is your annual household income?
- Less than $19,999
- $20,000–$39,999
- $40,000–$59,999
- $60,000–$79,999
- $80,000 or more

Note: The options listed for an income question will depend largely on your local area and your research question. If your library is located in an area with a low median income, the options could include more granularity at the bottom of the income scale.

EDUCATION

What is the highest level of school that you have completed or the highest degree that you have received?
- Less than high school degree
- High school degree or equivalent (e.g., GED)
- Some college, but no degree
- Associate's degree
- Bachelor's degree
- Graduate degree

LOCATION

If geographic location is relevant to your research, the questions and options depend on the type of library and target audience. For example, a public library with multiple branches may ask respondents about their neighborhood of residence. A corporate or government library serving multiple sites may ask about office location. A college or university serving commuter or online students may ask for ZIP code, county name, or simply "on-campus, online, or hybrid status."

Appendix B

Sample Questions About Services

Please rate your satisfaction with the library's customer service:
- Extremely satisfied
- Satisfied
- Dissatisfied
- Extremely dissatisfied
- No basis for judgment

The library offers services in several locations. How frequently do you use:

	Frequently	Occasionally	Not at all	I'm not familiar with this
Library Web site	○	○	○	○
Chat/instant message	○	○	○	○
Circulation desk	○	○	○	○
Reference desk	○	○	○	○
Special collections and archives	○	○	○	○

Please tell us if you have ever used any of the following services, and choose the option that best describes your opinion of the service.

| | Have you used this service? | | If yes, how would you rate your experience? | | | |
	Yes	No	Extremely satisfied	Satisfied	Dissatisfied	Extremely dissatisfied
Research assistance	○	○	○	○	○	○
Interlibrary Loan	○	○	○	○	○	○
Equipment checkout	○	○	○	○	○	○
Study/meeting rooms	○	○	○	○	○	○

Appendix C

Sample Questions About Spaces

How frequently do you visit the library building?
- More than once a week
- Less than once a week
- A few times a month
- A few times a semester
- Rarely

When you visit the library, about how much time do you estimate you spend in the building doing any of the following?

	5+ hours	3–4 hours	1–2 hours	Less than an hour	I don't do this in the library
Reading, studying, or working alone	○	○	○	○	○
Studying or working in a group	○	○	○	○	○
Taking a break	○	○	○	○	○

I am satisfied with my ability to do the following in the library:

	Strongly agree	Agree	Neither agree nor disagree	Disagree	Strongly disagree
Locate things I need	O	O	O	O	O
Study/work/research with others	O	O	O	O	O
Find a space appropriate for my needs	O	O	O	O	O
Communicate with others	O	O	O	O	O
Find vending machines	O	O	O	O	O
Get my work done	O	O	O	O	O
Use a computer workstation	O	O	O	O	O
Print	O	O	O	O	O

Which of the following best describes your feelings about these aspects of the library?

	Extremely satisfied	Somewhat satisfied	Somewhat dissatisfied	Extremely dissatisfied	No basis for judgment
Lighting	O	O	O	O	O
Options to purchase food or beverages	O	O	O	O	O
Access to electrical outlets	O	O	O	O	O
Furniture	O	O	O	O	O
Space for quiet study	O	O	O	O	O

	Extremely satisfied	Somewhat satisfied	Somewhat dissatisfied	Extremely dissatisfied	No basis for judgment
Space for group projects	○	○	○	○	○
Décor	○	○	○	○	○
Room temperature	○	○	○	○	○
Restrooms	○	○	○	○	○

How would you describe the library as a place? (Select all that apply.)
- Depressing
- Friendly
- Relaxed
- Serious
- Tense
- Tranquil
- Uncomfortable
- Upbeat
- Other, please list: _____

Thinking of the last time you were in the library, how did you feel? (Select all that apply.)
- Alert
- Calm
- Confused
- Distracted
- Efficient
- Empowered
- Focused
- Lost
- Overwhelmed
- Relaxed

- Sleepy
- Slow
- Smart

Have you been diagnosed with a disability?
- Yes
- No

DISPLAY LOGIC

If "Have you been diagnosed with a disability?" = Yes

How would you describe your disability? Select all that apply.
- A sensory impairment (related to vision or hearing)
- A mobility impairment or limitation
- A learning disability (e.g., ADHD, dyslexia)
- A mental health condition
- A disability or impairment not listed above

Thinking about using the library to get your work done, what are the obstacles that you experience? Please describe.

_____

_____

How do you feel about your safety when visiting the library?

	Concerned	Somewhat Concerned	Not Concerned
Arriving	○	○	○
Departing during the day	○	○	○
Departing at night	○	○	○
Studying during the day	○	○	○
Studying at night	○	○	○

DISPLAY LOGIC

If "How do you feel about your safety when visiting the library?"
= Concerned

Or "How do you feel about your safety when visiting the library?"
= Somewhat concerned

Please tell us more about your safety concerns, including the general location(s) and time(s) of day that you are concerned for your safety.

_____

_____

Appendix D

Sample Questions About Communication

When you use the library Web site, are you able to find what you need?
- Always
- Most of the time
- Sometimes
- Rarely
- Never

Do you receive information from the library using any of the following communication tools? (Select all that apply.)
- Library home page
- Library news blog
- Library Facebook page
- Library Twitter feed
- Signs in the library
- E-mails from the library about borrowing or borrowing services
- Library Guides
- Library newsletter
- Electronic displays

How would you prefer to receive announcements and information about library services, events, and tools? *Rank these methods, with 1 being most preferable and 6 being least preferable.*

_____ E-mail

_____ Library Web site

_____ Facebook or Twitter

_____ Flyers/signs around campus

_____ Plasma screens on the first floor of the library

_____ Talking to a library employee

How much information do you feel you get about each of the following?

	Too much	Just enough	Not enough
Research assistance	○	○	○
Programs and events	○	○	○
Books, databases, equipment, and other tools offered by the library	○	○	○

Note: This is an example of a question specifically designed for instructors in primary, secondary, or postsecondary education.

How well informed do you feel about the following?

	Always	Sometimes	Never
Library services	○	○	○
Databases and subscriptions	○	○	○
Information literacy instruction	○	○	○
Programs and events	○	○	○
How to request additions to the library collection	○	○	○

Appendix E

Sample Questions About Collections

To what extent do you believe that the following library collections meet your needs or interests?

	Very well	Somewhat	Not at all	Not applicable to my needs/ interests
Books	○	○	○	○
Scholarly/peer-reviewed journals	○	○	○	○
Popular magazines or newspapers	○	○	○	○
Databases	○	○	○	○
DVDs and streaming videos	○	○	○	○
Music recordings	○	○	○	○
Musical scores	○	○	○	○
Archival resources	○	○	○	○
Government documents	○	○	○	○

Do you ever use the library collection for any of the following? (Select all that apply.)

- ☐ Books to read for pleasure
- ☐ Movies for entertainment
- ☐ Music for entertainment
- ☐ Books for children or young adults
- ☐ Magazines/periodicals for personal use
- ☐ Board games

When you find that an item is not available at the library, what do you do? (Select all that apply.)

- ☐ Request the item through Interlibrary Loan
- ☐ Contact the library to ask for help
- ☐ Give up and find something else
- ☐ Buy a personal copy of the item with my own money
- ☐ Ask the library to buy the item
- ☐ See if the item is available from another local library
- ☐ Ask a friend
- ☐ Google it

Think about the following kinds of information that you might use in research. Which format do you prefer?

	Electronic	Print	Either
Books	○	○	○
Articles	○	○	○
Images	○	○	○
Maps	○	○	○

Appendix F

Sample Programming Questions

How many library programs or events have you attended in the last 6 months?

- More than 6
- 4–6
- 2–3
- 1
- None

How did you hear about the program that you attended?

- Library Web site
- Facebook event
- Local news media
- Another organization
- Library newsletter
- E-mail promotion
- Friend
- Other:

Please select the top **two** barriers that prevent you from attending library programs.

- I don't have time
- I cannot attend programs during the day

- I cannot attend programs in the evening
- I am not interested in the topics
- I do not have anyone to care for my family when I'm out
- I don't know if I can bring my children
- The library is too far from my home
- The library is difficult to get to
- The library makes me uncomfortable

Thinking about the future, would you consider attending any of the following library programs?

	Very likely	Somewhat likely	Not at all likely
Book group	○	○	○
Hands-on technology workshop	○	○	○
Expert speaker	○	○	○
Movie and discussion	○	○	○
Genealogy class	○	○	○
Local history event	○	○	○
Life skills classes (e.g., finances, nutrition)	○	○	○
Voter education	○	○	○
Musical or theatrical event	○	○	○

Appendix G

Additional Resources

TO LEARN MORE ABOUT RESEARCH METHODS

Connaway, Lynn Silipigni, and Marie Radford. *Research Methods in Library and Information Science*. 6th ed. Santa Barbara, CA: Libraries Unlimited, 2017.

Dando, Priscille. *Say It with Data: A Concise Guide to Making Your Case and Getting Results*. Chicago: ALA Editions, 2014.

Dillman, Don A., Jolene D. Smyth, and Leah Melani Christian. *Internet, Phone, Mail, and Mixed-Mode Surveys: The Tailored Design Method*. 4th ed. Hoboken, NJ: Wiley, 2014.

Harris, David F. *The Complete Guide to Writing Questionnaires: How to Get Better Information for Better Decisions*. Durham, NC: I&M Press, 2014.

Saldaña, Johnny. *The Coding Manual for Qualitative Researchers*. 3rd ed. Los Angeles: SAGE, 2016.

TO LEARN MORE ABOUT DECISION FATIGUE

Baumeister, Roy F., and John Tierney. *Willpower: The Rediscovery of Humans' Greatest Strength*. New York: Penguin Press, 2011.

Tierney, John. "To Choose Is to Lose." *The New York Times Magazine* (August 21, 2011): 33–37, 46.

TO LEARN MORE ABOUT DESIGN THINKING

Brown, Tim, and Barry Katz. *Change by Design: How Design Thinking Transforms Organizations and Inspires Innovation.* New York: Harper Business, 2009.

Brown, Tim, and Roger Martin. "Design for Action." *Harvard Business Review* 93, no. 9 (2015): 56–64.

Hasso Plattner Institute of Design. "Get Started with Design Thinking." Stanford University. Accessed June 1, 2018, from https://dschool .stanford.edu/resources/getting-started-with-design-thinking.

References

American Marketing Association. "Definition of Marketing." Accessed June 26, 2018, from https://www.ama.org/AboutAMA/Pages/Definition -of-Marketing.aspx.

Association of Research Libraries. "Survey FAQs: How Is the Libqual+® Survey Constructed and Conducted?" Accessed June 26, 2018, from https://www.libqual.org/about/about_survey/faq_survey.

Brown, Tim. "Design Thinking." *Harvard Business Review* 86, no. 6 (2008): 84–92.

Brown, Tim, and Roger Martin. "Design for Action." *Harvard Business Review* 93, no. 9 (2015): 56–64.

Connaway, Lynn Silipigni, and Marie Radford. *Research Methods in Library and Information Science*. 6th ed. Santa Barbara, CA: Libraries Unlimited, 2017.

Crawford, Scott D., Mick P. Couper, and Mark J. Lamias. "Web Surveys— Perceptions of Burden." *Social Science Computer Review* 19, no. 2 (2001): 146–162.

Dando, Priscille. *Say It with Data: A Concise Guide to Making Your Case and Getting Results*. Chicago: ALA Editions, 2014.

Dillman, Don A., Jolene D. Smyth, and Leah Melani Christian. *Internet, Phone, Mail, and Mixed-Mode Surveys: The Tailored Design Method*. 4th ed. Hoboken, NJ: Wiley, 2014.

Dowling, Brendan. "Cris Beam on Empathy's Ability to Be Both Personal and Exemplary." *Public Libraries Online*. Accessed March 29, 2018, from http://publiclibrariesonline.org/2018/03/beam/.

Halpern, Rebecca, Christopher Eaker, John Jackson, and Daina Bouquin. "#ditchthesurvey: Expanding Methodological Diversity in LIS Research." *In the Library with the Lead Pipe*. Accessed March 11, 2015, from

http://www.inthelibrarywiththeleadpipe.org/2015/ditchthesurvey
-expanding-methodological-diversity-in-lis-research/.

Harris, David F. *The Complete Guide to Writing Questionnaires: How to
Get Better Information for Better Decisions.* Durham, NC: I&M Press,
2014.

Hayden, Carla D. "Dr. Carla D. Hayden on the Need for Constant Change in
Libraries." Interview by Skip Prichard. *Next*, OCLC, December 5, 2017,
video, 10:26. Accessed July 17, 2018, from http://www.oclc.org/blog
/main/dr-carla-d-hayden-on-the-need-for-constant-change-in-libraries/.

Johnson, Allan G. *The Blackwell Dictionary of Sociology: A User's Guide
to Sociological Language.* 2nd ed. Malden, MA: Blackwell Publishers,
2000.

Krosnick, Jon A., Allyson L. Holbrook, Matthew K. Berent, Richard T. Car-
son, W. Michael Hanemann, Raymond J. Kopp, and Robert Cameron
Mitchell. "The Impact of 'No Opinion' Response Options on Data
Quality." *Public Opinion Quarterly* 66, no. 3 (2001): 371–403, http://dx
.doi.org/10.1086/341394.

Langer, Gary, Gregory Holyk, Chad Kiewiet De Jong, and Sofi Sinozich.
2016. "Clinton, Trump at Campaign's End: Still Close—and Still Unpop-
ular (Poll)." *ABC News*, November 7, 2016, 7:00 a.m. EST. Accessed
July 17, 2018, from https://abcnews.go.com/Politics/clinton-trump
-campaigns-end-close-unpopular-poll/story?id=43344414.

McGeeney, Kyley, and H. Yanna Yan. "Text Message Notification for Web
Surveys." *Pew Research Center*, September 7, 2016. Accessed July 17,
2018, from http://www.pewresearch.org/2016/09/07/text-message
-notification-for-web-surveys/.

McKee, Robert. *Story: Substance, Structure, Style, and the Principles of
Screenwriting.* New York: ReganBooks, 1997.

Mercer, Andrew, Claudia Deane, and Kyley McGeeney. "Why 2016 Election Polls Missed Their Mark." *Pew Research Center*, November 9,
2016. Accessed July 17, 2018, from http://www.pewresearch.org/fact
-tank/2016/11/09/why-2016-election-polls-missed-their-mark/.

Mercer, Andrew, Arnold Lau, and Courtney Kennedy. "For Weighting Online
Opt-in Samples, What Matters Most?" *Pew Research Center*, Janu-
ary 26, 2018. Accessed July 17, 2018, from http://www.pewresearch.org
/2018/01/26/for-weighting-online-opt-in-samples-what-matters-most/.

Perrin, Andrew, and Jingjing Jiang. "About a Quarter of U.S. Adults Say
They Are 'Almost Constantly' Online." *Pew Research Center*, March 14,
2018. Accessed July 17, 2018, from http://www.pewresearch.org/fact
-tank/2018/03/14/about-a-quarter-of-americans-report-going-online
-almost-constantly/.

Poels, Karolien, and Siegfried Dewitte. "How to Capture the Heart? Reviewing 20 Years of Emotion Measurement in Advertising." *Journal of*

Advertising Research 46, no. 1 (2006): 18–37, https://doi.org/10.1177 /0539018405058216.

Polkinghorne, Donald. *Narrative Knowing and the Human Sciences.* Albany: State University of New York Press, 1988.

Saldaña, Johnny. *The Coding Manual for Qualitative Researchers.* 3rd ed. Los Angeles: SAGE, 2016.

Scherer, Klaus R. "What Are Emotions? And How Can They Be Measured?" *Social Science Information* 44, no. 4 (2005): 695–729, https://doi.org /10.1177/0539018405058216.

Schmidt, Aaron, and Amanda Etches. *Useful, Usable, Desirable: Applying User Experience Design to Your Library.* Chicago: ALA Editions, 2014.

Singer, Eleanor. "Survey Incentives," in *The Palgrave Handbook of Survey Research*, eds. David L. Vannette and John A. Krosnick. Cham, Switzerland: Palgrave Macmillan, 405–415, 2018.

Steimer, Sarah. "What Nonprofits Can Learn About Customer Experience from the Met's Rebrand." *Marketing News* 52, no. 3 (March 2018): 6–8.

Sue, Valerie M., and Lois A. Ritter. *Conducting Online Surveys.* 2nd ed. Thousand Oaks, CA: SAGE, 2012.

Tierney, John. "To Choose Is to Lose." *The New York Times Magazine* (August 21, 2011): 33–37, 46.

Tonetto, Leandro Miletto, and Pieter M. A. Desmet. "Natural Language in Measuring User Emotions: A Qualitative Approach to Quantitative Survey-Based Emotion Measurement." *Out of Control: Proceedings of the 8th International Conference on Design and Emotion, London, UK, 11–14 September 2012* (2012). Accessed July 17, 2018, from uuid:88ba101e-dfb5-4801-88d1-98d216a4eba5.

Vohs, Kathleen D., Roy F. Baumeister, Brandon J. Schmeichel, Jean M. Twenge, Noelle M. Nelson, Dianne M. Tice, and Charles S. Carver. "Making Choices Impairs Subsequent Self-Control: A Limited-Resource Account of Decision Making, Self-Regulation, and Active Initiative." *Journal of Personality and Social Psychology* 94, no. 5 (May 2008): 883–898. https://doi.org/10.1037/0022-3514.94.5.883.

Index

About the Authors

ROBIN MILLER is an associate professor and assessment and instruction librarian at the University of Wisconsin–Eau Claire, in Eau Claire, Wisconsin. She received a Master of Science in library and information science from the University of Illinois at Urbana-Champaign.

KATE HINNANT is an associate professor and head of instruction and communication at the University of Wisconsin–Eau Claire, in Eau Claire, Wisconsin. She received a Master of Science in library and information science from the University of Illinois at Urbana-Champaign and a Master of Fine Arts in creative writing from Purdue University in West Lafayette, Indiana. She is also a coauthor of *Maximizing the One-Shot: Connecting Library Instruction with the Curriculum.*